OTHER BOOKS AND VIDEOS
BY RONALD J. FIELDS ON FIELDS

Fields, Ronald J., *W. C. Fields: A Life on Film*. New York: St. Martin's, 1984.

Fields, W. C. (edited by Ronald J. Fields), *W. C. Fields by Himself: His Intended Autobiography*. Englewood Cliffs: Prentice-Hall, 1973.

W. C. Fields Straight Up, W. C. Fields Productions, 1986. Emmy Award Winner

NEVER GIVE A SUCKER AN EVEN BREAK

W.C. FIELDS ON BUSINESS

RONALD FIELDS
with SHAUN O'L. HIGGINS

PRENTICE HALL PRESS

Library of Congress Cataloging-in-Publication Data

Fields, Ronald J.
    Never give a sucker an even break : W. C. Fields on management / Ronald Fields,
    Shaun O'L Higgins.
        p. cm.
    Includes bibliographical references and index.
    ISBN 0-7352-0056-4 (cloth)
      1. Fields, W. C., 1879-1946. 2. Management. I. Higgins, Shaun. II. Title.
    HD38.F515   1999
    658—dc21   99-049404
                                                 CIP

Acquisitions Editor: *Tom Power*
Production Editor: *Eve Mossman*
Formatting: *Robyn Beckerman*
Interior Design: *Tom Nery*

©*2000 by Ronald J. Fields*

*All rights reserved. No part of this book may be reproduced in any form or by any means,
without permission in writing from the publisher.*

*The right to use the name, likeness, photographs, and materials of W. C. Fields were granted to
Ronald J. Fields for the purposes of this book and advertising same by the legal rights holder
W. C. Fields Productions, Inc.*

Printed in the United States of America

10 9 8 7 6 5 4 3 2 1

ISBN 0-7352-0056-4

PRENTICE HALL PRESS
Paramus, NJ 07652

On the World Wide Web at http://www.phdirect.com

With unabashed love,
I dedicate this book to my wife, Pamela, my daughter,
Chelsea, and my son, Alexander!

ACKNOWLEDGMENTS

First of all, I must give a hearty handclasp and a great thanks to my grandfather, W. C. Fields.

Next I want to thank my brothers and sister, Bill, Everett, Harriet and Allen for their support and their bestowing of the rights from our family corporation, W. C. FIELDS PRODUCTIONS, INC., to me to use the photos and the likeness of W. C.

Shaun O'L. Higgins has my heartiest thanks for his dedication to business and W. C. and for his relentless good cheer and professional approach. It was a pleasure to work with him.

A salute goes to Trent Price who agented this book.

A martini toast goes to Jeff Lotman for his support of my work and his enthusiastic confabulations with Yvette Romero and Sally Hertz of Prentice Hall in helping promote this tome. And, of course, a clink of the glass goes to Yvette and Sally for their constant enthusiasm for this book as well. Thanks!

A hearty handclasp goes to the editor of this book Tom Power, who did a splendid juggling job in organizing the construction of this work.

And a toast clink to Eve Mossman a friend from my first-book-days at Prentice Hall and a friend from this-book-days at Prentice Hall.

A hearty handclasp goes to Barry Richardson for his insightful editing and wonderful developmental work on this book.

VIII

NEVER GIVE A
SUCKER AN EVEN
BREAK
*W. C. Fields on
Business*

A clink of the martini glass goes to Tom Nery for his fabulous design and to Robyn Beckerman for her excellent execution of the same.

A hearty handclasp and a clink of the martini glass goes to James Curtis, the fine author and good friend for his help and his inspiring in-depth research on my grandfather for his upcoming biography of W. C.

A special thanks and the heartiest of handclasps goes to Ted Wioncek, the President of W. C. Fields's official fan club. The toast to you goes for keeping and cherishing the memory of my grandfather.

And finally, a clink of the glass, a toast, a sip, a hearty handclasp, and hugs and kisses to the trio to whom I've dedicated this book, my wife, Pam, my daughter Chelsea, and my son, Alex.

CONTENTS

NEVER GIVE A
SUCKER AN EVEN
BREAK
*W. C. Fields on
Business*

INTRODUCTION

TIRED OF PC?
TRY W. C.!

"YOU CAN'T CHEAT AN HONEST MAN"

W. C. FIELDS A MANAGEMENT GURU? "POPPYCOCK!" you say?

Sure, Fields is considered one of the greatest comic geniuses of all time; and, yes, his life was the stuff of legend; and, certainly, his one-liners—delivered in his unique style—are famous throughout the world:

- "Never give a sucker an even break!"
- "You can't cheat an honest man!"
- "Never smarten up a chump!"
- "Anything worth having is worth cheating for."
- "You can fool half the people all of the time . . . and that's enough to make a good living."
- "Even a worm will turn!"

Fields was a great entertainer, but a management coach? "Balderdash!" you say.

XII
NEVER GIVE A
SUCKER AN EVEN
BREAK
*W. C. Fields on
Business*

Didn't Fields portray heavy-drinking slackers, mumbling malcontents, unscrupulous pettifoggers, four-flushing con artists, and petty tyrants? Didn't he claim to hate kids and dogs? Didn't his characters thrive by fleecing human sheep? What kind of a role model is that for the politically correct workplace? What possibly can be learned from such a curmudgeonly, bilious, bibulous rapscallion?

The answers to those questions, in order, are (1) "Yes, he did," (2) "Yes, he did," (3) "Yes, sometimes," (4) "He's a model you can learn from," and (5) "Plenty!"

Welcome to W. C. University where the lessons are taught by Fields and a faculty of alter egos: Larson E. Whipsnade, The Great McGonigle, Egbert Sousé, Cuthbert J. Twillie, Professor Eustace P. McGargle, Samuel Bisbee, T. Frothingell Bellows, Ambrose Wolfinger, Wilkins Micawber, Commodore Orlando Jackson, Harold Bissonette (rhymes with Chardonnay), Sheriff "Honest John" Hoxley, Augustus Q. Winterbottom, Professor Quail, Charles Bogle, Mahatma Kane Jeeves, Otis Cribblecobbis, and Rollo LaRue.

W. C. Fields was a comic genius, in part, because he could find humor in situations most of us pay little attention to or dismiss as routine—situations such as buying a stamp, filing a piece of paper, holding a sale, playing a round of golf, or going to the dentist. Fields also recognized the weak points in conventional wisdom, and, like Scott Adams's "Dilbert," he highlighted the absurdities of work and the workplace. He knew how to draw a laugh at the same time he made his audiences think, "Yeah, I've seen people do that before, sure was stupid." Fields addressed nearly every situation afflicting the human condition.

No doubt if W. C. were alive today, he'd find lots to poke fun at in our offices. He'd probably see them as soul deadening, politically correct, humorless seas of cubicles. Oh sure, he'd know that many of those cubicles are filled with hardworking, dedicated people who deserve to stand out. But he would also know that others are filled with bureaucratic bunglers who, like many of the characters he portrayed, wouldn't have much regard for customers or fellow workers, let alone the company that employs them. Certainly, W. C. would find a few Micawbers (probably much less likable ones than the character he played in *David Copperfield*). Every office has them: mystic thinkers who believe that something will magically "turn up" to solve their problems. (How do you get Micawbers focused on creating their own luck?) And Fields would find in those cubicles a whole array of other dysfunctionals: the slackers, well poisoners, weasels, "petite satraps," and nincompoops, with whom you, unfortunately, have to deal on a daily basis.

Throughout *Never Give a Sucker an Even Break*, we use W. C. and his alter egos to illustrate business problems. We also use examples from Fields's life and the business world to show you how to avoid pitfalls as you help your company grow revenues, reduce costs, deal with crises, and manage its image. You'll also get insights into achieving your personal goals both within and outside the workplace.

We've already told you a bit about Fields, and chances are you wouldn't be reading this book if you didn't already have some appreciation for his comedy. But even if you've seen the films, you may not know much about the man behind the characters, so here's a short version of his life and career:

XIV

NEVER GIVE A
SUCKER AN EVEN
BREAK
*W. C. Fields on
Business*

W. C. Fields was born William Claude Dukenfield just outside Philadelphia on January 29, 1880. Fields often described his family as "poor but dishonest." Neither part of the description was precise, but the line always got a laugh— and comedians live for laughs. Fields's father, James Dukenfield, was a hard-working English emigrant and a decorated Union Army veteran of the Civil War. When the war ended, Dukenfield settled in Philadelphia, married Kate Felton, and became a wholesale vegetable merchant, a huckster. The Fields family was known for its idiosyncrasies of speech and voice. Prone to frequent colds, even young W. C. spoke with a gravelly voice. Mother Kate tended to mumble some of her remarks (much in the style W. C. would eventually adopt). Father James spoke with a pronounced Cockney accent, which was a frequent target of Kate's mumbling asides.

As the son of a merchant, W. C. learned early and first-hand the ins and outs of small business. At the tender age of 12 Fields got a job with a department store; later he worked (make that fought) with his father as a huckster walking the streets of Philadelphia selling fruits and vegetables from a horse-drawn cart. Finally, at the age of 18, William Claude broke into vaudeville as a juggler—but only after purloining enough of his father's fruits and vegetables to make an act. Soon after hitting the stage, he changed his name from Dukenfield to "Field" and then "Fields" (managers were adding the "s" anyway, so he decided to go with it).

Years later, in his movies, Fields often played a manager, though seldom a good one: In *The Pharmacist*, he ran a drugstore; in *The Dentist*, he managed a dental office; in *The Old*

Fashioned Way, he managed a theater troupe; in *You Can't Cheat an Honest Man,* he ran a circus. When he died on Christmas Day 1946, W. C. Fields was among the best-known celebrities in the world. He had brought laughter to millions, first during 17 hugely successful years in vaudeville, followed by 15 years of Broadway appearances and more than 40 roles in motion pictures. Fields never let a technological development block his career path. He not only managed the transition from vaudeville to Broadway, but also the transitions from stage to screen, silent screen to "talkies," and from "talkies" to radio.

Unfortunately, W. C. Fields, my grandfather, died a few years before I was born, but reading his letters, watching his films, and studying his life have shown me what a great teacher he could be.

So watch W. C. on the screen, listen to his radio performances, and read about how he skillfully managed his own career. Here's a preview of some of things you'll learn as you read on.

BRANDING

There are hundreds of famous comedians, but only one W. C. Fields. Fields was (and is) a brand. He consciously established, extended, and protected his image. Procter & Gamble couldn't have done it better. W. C. (Uncle Bill to his friends) also played an early part in the role of "product mentions," helping promote the brands of Chesterfield and Lucky Strike cigarettes, Blatz beer, and Chase & Sanborn coffee. Whether you are building a brand for your company or trying to brand

XVI
_____

NEVER GIVE A
SUCKER AN EVEN
BREAK
W. C. Fields on
Business

yourself as a winner, Fields can help. His life was full of examples of ways to make yourself a brand so you can differentiate yourself from your "prairie-dogging" neighbors, stand out from the pack, and win promotions.

THINKING

You're only as good as your brain and the ideas it produces. Whenever Fields got an idea—and he got lots of them—he wrote it down so it wouldn't be forgotten. Later he would reconsider the idea, discarding it or developing it until he had something that would work. He also tested his ideas on others before trying them out on his audiences, a practice he discusses in letters to his fellow comedians. W. C. knew that having an idea was not enough; an idea had to be polished, tested, and reworked until it was perfected.

ENTERPRISE

W. C. knew how to hustle, and we aren't just talking about poolrooms and card tables. There's a wonderful example from W. C.'s youth: Fields shows up to apply for a job at the Strawbridge & Clothier department store in Philadelphia. Hundreds of applicants are waiting outside S&C hoping for an interview. A gust of wind blows over a sign advertising the position. Fields grabs the sign and rushes it inside to the personnel office. The company is so impressed with his enterprise, they give him the job on the spot.

COMMUNICATION AND COURTESY

Fields was a prolific correspondent, and he wrote classic complaint letters, thank-you letters, and letters soliciting roles. E-mail may make it easier to send an effective message, but it doesn't make it easier to write one. This is one area in which Fields offers countless examples on how to do it "write." (Once in a letter he paraphrased Mae West and invited a lawyer to "Come up and sue me sometime.")

Fields also knew what professional thoughtfulness and courtesy were about. The mean-spirited, credit-grabbing character we see on the screen was a very different man from the W. C. Fields who wrote dozens of spontaneous letters to fellow comedians, praising their latest routines. When Fields saw good work, he credited it. As a result he seldom was denied the right to build on the good work of others as a means of improving his own routines.

JUGGLING PAPERWORK

In *The Man on the Flying Trapeze*, Fields's character, Ambrose Wolfinger, plays a corporate "Memory Expert." In addition to helping the president of his company remember personal information on visiting business associates, Wolfinger reigns over a mountain of papers on the messiest desk imaginable. However, he controls this chaos with his impenetrable filing system. In one great scene, Wolfinger is asked to locate a particular document. He reaches into his pile of parchment and pulls out a piece of paper . . . the wrong one. "Drat!" He pauses, reaches into the mess again, and withdraws the desired report. "Eureka!" He looks at it, waits a beat, then delivers the punchline. "Ah," he

XVIII

NEVER GIVE A
SUCKER AN EVEN
BREAK
*W. C. Fields on
Business*

says, "misfiled!" Fields proves here and elsewhere that messy desks are not necessarily the product of messy minds.

DIFFICULT PEOPLE

Fields worked with the best comedians of his day. When they appeared together, both Fields and the other comedian required equal billing and an equal chance to show their skills and get their laughs. You think your peers are tough competitors for corporate attention, imagine competing for the limelight with Charlie McCarthy, Mae West, or Baby LeRoy. Let Professor Fields show you how to hold your own in any boardroom or brainstorming session.

OFFICE POLITICS

In his finest screen role, Fields (as Mr. Micawber in *David Copperfield*) dealt with one of the great white-collar villains of all time: the oily, deceitful, and falsely "'umble" Uriah Heep. But Heep wasn't the only backstabber Fields confronted, and some of his best lines deal with office politics. If young Turks surround you in your office, you can take comfort in Fields's reminder that "they're only young snakes—even if they bite you, you wouldn't die."

TIMING

Timing is everything—on stage, in business, and in life. Fields was a master of comedic timing and of time itself. For example, he liked to sleep late, so he chose a career that enabled him to match his energies to his physical needs. His skits show his familiarity with the countless excuses found for missing appointments and deadlines (our favorite is "I'd have been here sooner, only I got stuck on a piece of chewing gum"). Fields's work provides countless examples showing that, in comedy, *what* you say is important, *how* you say it is more important, but *when* you say it can be the most important of all. W. C.'s understanding of "preparation, pause, and punch" can be as critical to business presentations as it is to telling a good joke.

ADAPTABILITY

Got lemons? Make lemonade! Fields was a master of doing this. In his younger days he incorporated a string of patter in his juggling act, which limited him to national tours. He wanted worldwide fame, so he turned his act into a silent, comic juggling act and soon he was billed as The World's Greatest Juggler. In another stroke of brilliance, he designed a particularly difficult juggling trick so that if the trick didn't work, his calculated reaction to the flub brought on howls of laughter, which turned his serious juggling routine into a world-acclaimed comic juggling act. Applying Fields's ability to assess weaknesses and anticipate problems has myriad applications in the workplace.

INVENTION AND CREATIVITY

Fields's creativity wasn't limited to his scripts and his roles. He once invented a paper-towel dispenser and came up with ideas for dozens of humorous pseudoinventions, such as the

Necktie Soup Set (it contained six ties that matched in color and design the types of soup that might be spilled on them). Fields never wasted an idea. If an idea wasn't practical as a real invention, he would incorporate it into his comedy routines and films.

LEADERSHIP

In *Million Dollar Legs*, Fields plays the President of Klopstokia, a mythical European country with an empty treasury, but teeming with undiscovered, world-class athletes. Fields is literally the country's strongman—in fact, he's its strongest man, an Olympic-quality weight lifter. Produced during the Depression, the movie is filled with scenes in which President Fields exhibits several leadership traits. He's candid ("What this country needs is money!"). He knows how to select subordinates (he finds the only adviser in the country immune to the charms of a blond-bombshell spy played by Lyda Roberti). He can out-armwrestle every member of his disloyal cabinet, and he knows how, literally, to toot his own horn when occasion demands (when he makes his formal entrances, he accompanies himself as a one-man band).

BUDGETING

Fields wrote a great comic essay entitled "How to Beat a Budget." It was supposed to be a chapter in W. C.'s 1941 book, *Fields for President*, but for some reason it suffered an editor's scalpel. Basically, you start with seven jars and then you . . . well, find out how Fields can help you think through department budgets in Chapter 7.

These are just a few of the things you'll learn—along with tips on managing crisis, handling change, improving your teamwork, and mastering the art of delegation.

As W. C. once said, "There comes a time in the affairs of men when you must grab the bull by the tail and face the situation." So read on and you'll soon be able to "face the situation" by doing a better job of managing your work, your employees, and your career. And you'll get more than a few laughs along the way.

"How come you talk so loud?" W. C.: "I've got to talk loud, I'm the Sheriff."
Maybe not the greatest advice on heading up business, but at least it's funny.

CHAPTER ONE

LEADERSHIP SECRETS

THE BUSINESS SECTIONS OF BOOKSTORES ARE FILLED with titles on leadership, the hottest corporate topic of the past decade. These books come in three basic types:

TYPE I: *General theory and practice of leadership.* Business-school professors, including great masters such as Warren Bennis, Peter Drucker, John P. Kotter, and Michael Maccoby, usually write these books. They are authoritative sourcebooks filled with valuable information as well as practical guidance on leadership. They are the foundations for all other books on the topic.

TYPE II: *Organizational leadership.* These books focus primarily on the application of leadership principles to achieve change and create a commitment to organizations and their missions. They are often written by business profs, CEOs, and consultants who have devoted their lives to studying this single topic. They build on the theories of the masters, applying them in the context of helping organizations achieve consensus. These usually run about 300 pages and are set in standard type sizes.

TYPE III: *Personal leadership and celebrity role-model books.* These books invariably are built around "the secrets" of an historic (sometimes fictional) figure: Caesar, Patton, Bismarck, Napoleon—even W. C. Fields! Type III books tend to be the shortest in the genre. They focus on how to be a leader, rather than on a corporation's need to have leadership. Type III books are the most common type of leadership book and a specialty of many popular business writers. Type III books are often purchased by people who have an interest in the historic or fictional character on which they are based and with whom the buyer identifies. (So we assume as you hold this book on Fields in one hand you have a martini in the other!)

Regardless of which of the three types of leadership book you prefer, the advice you'll find boils down to mastering the magnificent dozen traits:

1. You must want to lead.

2. You must have a plan and passionately believe in it.

3. You must work hard.

4. You must have at least some talent.

5. You must want to succeed.

6. You must be willing to make personal sacrifices.

7. You must put together a good team to back you up.

8. You must have a thick skin.

9. You must be articulate.

10. You must be able to inspire commitment in others.

11. You must be able to bounce back from setbacks.

12. You must be focused.

If you have the stuff of leadership within you, you already know most of this. So where does Fields fit in a chapter on leadership? We all know he hated *The Great Dictator* and its author-director-star Charlie Chaplin, whom he considered "nothing but a goddamn ballet dancer!" Fields did his own take on dictators in a jewel of a film he made in 1933.

In *Million Dollar Legs*, W. C. plays the president of Klopstokia, a mythical European country. Its major exports are goats and nuts. So are its major imports. So are its inhabitants. Despite all those goats and nuts, Klopstokia has an empty treasury and must find a way to fill it.

At a time when America was struggling through the Great Depression, Fields, as the president of Klopstokia, was facing similar economic woes. As the film begins, an enterprising American brush salesman has entered Klopstokia to open new markets. The salesman (played by Jack Oakie) meets the president's daughter and they fall in love at first sight. When the president demands to know his name, she tells him, "Well, I call him 'Sweetheart.'" And for the rest of the movie, Fields calls the salesman "Sweetheart." "Sweetheart" quickly figures out how Klopstokia can make money. It's 1932, the year of the first Los Angeles Olympic Games and Klopstokia turns out to be a nation of world-class athletes. Even the dictatorial president (Fields) is an athlete—a strongman who can hoist a 1,000-pound weight without breaking a sweat!

If the athletes can win the Olympics, the president will be a hero, his foes will be vanquished, his daughter will marry the man of her dreams, and the Klopstokian economy will be saved (the gold medals alone would fill Fort Knox!). Success in LA will definitely translate to success for the treasury. Fields decides his country will participate in the 1932 Games and appoints "Sweetheart" as the head coach. Decisive action! In Los Angeles the tiny country grabs all of the gold, Klopstokia is saved, and the brush salesman gets to marry the Prez's daughter. Now that's leadership!

Why use Genghis Khan's advice on leadership when you can draw on "Leadership Secrets of the President of Klopstokia?" Herewith some examples that bear a remarkable similarity to the advice you'll find in other books, but with a Fieldsian twist.

LEADERSHIP SECRETS OF THE PRESIDENT OF KLOPSTOKIA
(To be taken with a grain of salt!)

1. Say what you mean and be clear about it. Paraphrasing former vice president Thomas Marshall ("What this country needs is a good five-cent cigar!"), Klopstokia's president cuts to the chase about his own nation's plight: "What this country needs is money!"

2. Demand loyalty. Since everyone in his cabinet is disloyal, the President protects himself by demanding that they take a loyalty oath before each cabinet meeting. Being good subjects, they do so every time with their fingers crossed behind their backs.

3. Don't be afraid to toot your own horn—but economize when possible. No Marine Bands for the P of K; when he makes his formal entrances, a one-man band accompanies him—and he's the one man!

4. Demonstrate your desire to lead. The President wants to stay in the job so badly that he's ready to physically arm wrestle any upstart challenger—winner gets the job! Of course, after the plotters lose the arm-wrestling bout, they revisit their spying and sabotage.

5. Lead by example. As Klopstokia's strongest man, the President winds up entering the Olympics himself—and winning the weight-lifting contest.

6. Master the art of motivation. For the President this means clearly telling subordinates what is expected of them. For example, in his first assignment to Sweetheart (Jack Oakie), he makes the rewards/punishment outcomes clear: "Help me out of my trouble and you can marry my daughter; fail and I'll break every bone in your body."

7. Stay healthy. Arm wrestling maintains the President in office, so he can't afford to lose his strength. That means eating right. When he weakens, he knows it's time to get back to a healthy diet of . . . goat's milk . . . 80-proof goat's milk!

8. They ARE out to get you—and they aren't alone! The President knows his cabinet is plotting against him so he must question the motives of everyone around him. "I'm surrounded by spies," he says. "Sometimes I mistrust even myself."

9. Keep an eye on the bottom line. Klopstokia is $8 million in the hole. When the President asks Privy Councilor (and coach) Sweetheart to devise a plan to get the country out of debt, Fields explains the nation's financial plight succinctly: "We've got the zeros, now all we need is the 8!"

10. Knowledge is power. The President knows the value of education. Math, in particular, is helpful. "I should have gone to night school," he says, "I'd be able to add."

11. Delegate authority. Speaking by phone to a general who is plotting against him, he delegates power to the proper authority. "Put yourself under arrest!"

12. Be just! Show mercy!—But never be a sucker! When Sweetheart is hauled away by the palace guards, the President's daughter expresses her concern. "They won't hurt him, will they?" The President comforts her. "Only for about two hours, dear—then they'll kill him!"

As you watch *Million Dollar Legs,* you soon learn that the President maintains his power simply because he can lick any challenger. Force, not consensus, keeps him in office; indeed, the consensus seems to be almost unanimously against him. As Bill Gates might say, "Those were the good old days!" In the real world, persuasion and the power of your ideas will make you a leader.

From International House *Fields lands his Helicopter/Airplane called the Spirit of Brooklyn (a take-off of the very famous Spirit of St. Louis) through the open roof of the International House Hotel. He not only pilots his own resourceful invention, but he's resourceful on his feet. He tells the gathering he's looking for Kansas City, Kansas. They inform him he's in Wuhu, China, and that he must be lost. Fields: "Kansas City's lost . . . I am here."*

CHAPTER TWO

RESOURCEFULNESS

FIELDS'S CAREER TESTIFIES TO HIS RESOURCEFULNESS. He ad-libbed ad infinitum throughout his career with hilarious and profitable results. W. C. seized one opportunity after another. When it looked as if he had hit bottom in vaudeville, he jumped to Broadway and became a bigger star than ever. When his silent-film career went south and Broadway went bust because of the 1929 stock market crash, talking films saved his career. With resourcefulness, Fields hit the top in three different careers but is best known today for his talking movie career, which he did not begin until he was 50 years old!

Obviously, W. C. needed every bit of his wit to survive, and in our on-fire, profit-fueled economy, you don't need to be told that businesspeople today need resourcefulness even more than Fields did in his day. In the dizzyingly fast-paced environment of the Twenty-first Century, you must constantly devise ways and means of making things happen, and you have to be able to meet unexpected situations as they arise day in and day out. You must squeeze the most out of the things you have and be able to get your hands on the things you need and that does not include 80-proof pineapple juice. If all you've got to work with is lemons, you'd better learn how to make lemonade.

Fields had lots of native talent, but it came with some downside luggage. His greatest gift was that of knowing how to capitalize on his strengths and turn his negatives into positives.

Here are some examples:

- W. C.'s resourcefulness was evident when he first decided on a career in entertainment. Fields claimed he liked to sleep late, finding he worked best if he could spend mornings in bed. He told friends he chose a career in vaudeville because it let him match his job to his sleep cycle.

- W. C. began his career as a serious juggler in 1898 at the age of 18. Billing himself William Claude Dukenfield, Juggler Extraordinaire, he had been performing around the Philadelphia area for church bazaars and local fairs, but he got his first paying gig at a dump of a theater on the Atlantic City pier. He could not afford the typical Indian rubber balls and tuxedo of the serious jugglers of the time so he wore his own clothes. His name wouldn't fit on a marquee so managers put the knife to it and just like that, William

Claude Dukenfield, Juggler Extraordinaire, became W. C. Fields: Tramp Juggler. Soon, he learned that natural frustration over a missed trick made audiences howl. Seizing the opportunity, he became a comic juggler. Resourceful!

- Skyrocketing to fame while still in his teens, the young juggler was asked to join the most prestigious tour on earth, Keith Orpheum, for a national run. W. C. wanted the world and realizing that humor is culturally biased and difficult to translate from one language or culture to another, he reverted to a completely silent act, which never failed him before a foreign audience.

- In another brilliant adaptation, Fields developed a particularly difficult juggling trick—and insulated it from failure. Fields's pool-table trick sounds almost impossible: Using a pool cue, W. C. would poke the cue ball the length of a billiard table, causing it to hit the rail, fly in a high arc backward and land in his pocket! It was a stunning stunt even though he was aided by his customized, Brunswick-made trick table with rounded rails. Even with the special table, the trick frequently didn't work. So Fields designed his act accordingly: If the cue ball missed his pocket, it looked like an intentional flub. If he got the trick right the first time, the audience was astounded. If he missed the first time (or even a second time), he drew laughs as he searched for the ball and cued up again. By the time he landed the ball in his pocket the audience was already in there with him, rolling in tears and thoroughly impressed with both his juggling and his comedic skill.

- Later, when he left juggling to play comedy full time, Fields's routines concentrated on what he knew and the things he loved and hated. Golf, pool, tennis, and alcohol he liked. Kids, dogs, family, and his big nose he disliked. But he used them all. His first two movies—silents made in 1915—centered on pool and golf. In his talking films, allusions to the bottle and quips about his nose quickly became part of every Fields routine and made him more popular than ever. (As an example, Fields gave Charlie McCarthy the go sign to make the comment, "Isn't it true, Mr. Fields, that forty-two cars stopped at Hollywood and Vine waiting for your nose to turn green?")

Fields's resourcefulness was particularly apparent in his skill with ad-libs. The chemistry (or lack of it) between actors on stage can make or kill the best of scripts. If you've ever been in a play, you know that unexpected things happen: Part of the set collapses, a cell phone rings when it's not supposed to, a joke falls flat, a cast member misses a cue or forgets a line. Actors are trained to improvise when these things happen, but nobody has ever ad-libbed better than Fields. W. C. was not only quick-witted enough to cover most gaffes, he was also notorious for departing from scripts and spontaneously inserting his own lines—lines that were invariably better than the ones that had been written for him, including many he'd written originally himself. His ad-libs kept scripts fresh and kept fellow actors on their toes, forcing quick thinking from those around him. Those who couldn't keep up with him seldom got a second chance. Sometimes he tested his colleagues. For example, W. C created an unofficial team of people he used over and over in his films, a virtual Fields's Theatrical Troupe. One of the members was Grady Sutton. Sutton liked to tell the story of the time he sat at a table during a scene with an ad-libbing Fields. W. C. was unstoppable. He went on and on spouting wonderfully new lines until the frustrated director yelled "Cut!" The director then turned to Grady and said, "How come you're not saying your lines?" Sutton responded, "Because I don't know when to cut in. W. C.'s not saying *his* lines." Fields found the solution immediately, "Listen, Grady, I'm just going to keep talking. When you think I've said enough, just stop me."

TRANSLATING W. C. INTO BUSINESS TERMS

W. C.'s ability to assess his own weaknesses, anticipate problems, and ad-lib his way out of a boring script or unforeseen development is the stuff of legend, but what does it mean in the workplace? Let's look at some examples that illustrate W. C.'s style of resourcefulness in business.

EXAMPLE 1: *Overcoming a perceived liability.* Imagine you're an advertising agency located in a place that's not known as an advertising center. You're in Maine, or Washington State, or Nebraska. Most of your clients are local, but you have been doing great creative work and have recently picked up a couple of small national accounts. You have been unable, however, to land a huge client that's in your own backyard. The client you want is known worldwide, but considers you too small to handle its account. As an international company, the potential client believes it needs a major U.S. agency and that such agencies can be found only in a major advertising city. Consequently, it's chosen an agency in Los Angeles. How do you overcome its bias and show it that the best agency it can have is in its own hometown?

That's the situation that confronted Wieden & Kennedy, the remarkably creative Portland, Oregon advertising firm that now is one of the largest independently owned advertising agencies in the world, with global clients including Nike, Miller, Microsoft, ESPN, and Coca-Cola.

Nike was located in suburban Beaverton, Oregon. Portland, which has since become one of the hottest advertising cities in the country (they even have the American Advertising Museum there), was something of a backwater until the mid-eighties. Nike had started with W & K, but later decided that it needed to take its business to Los Angeles. W & K knew it could match any advertising produced anywhere in the world so it launched a full-frontal assault to recapture the Nike account. Their plan required them to turn their location—only a few miles from Nike headquarters—into an asset and show off W & K creativity at the same time. Among other efforts, W & K posted directional signs opposite the entry to the Nike plant. One sign pointed south and read "LOS ANGELES—959 MILES"; the other pointed north and read "WIEDEN & KENNEDY—10 MILES." Later, learning that Nike ad execs invariably stayed at a particular hotel in Los Angeles, the ad agency bought some wristwatches and had them delivered to the hotel around 8 P.M. Accompanying the watches was a card that read: "Time for a change: If you used WIEDEN & KENNEDY, you'd be home by now."

The W & K account execs kept up the assault, always using additional clever, nonoffensive ways to position themselves in the minds of the Nike buyers. Step-by-step, they built their case. Eventually they got an appointment, made their presentation, and landed the account, which they've held ever since.

EXAMPLE 2: *Making the miss a hit!*   When Fields designed his juggling trick for the stage, he knew the odds were against him. It worked in only about one out of every three times. But he made each miss look like a hit.

Here's what *The Spokesman-Review* newspaper in Spokane, Washington did when it hit a miss. The paper had posted a series of billboards around its community. One of the signs featured a giant inflatable of a man reading a newspaper. The inflatable board was designed for rotation at two-month intervals among four high-traffic locations. Shortly after being moved to the second location, however, vandals stole part of the sign, an inflated shoe that zipped onto the inflated leg of the figure. It would take weeks and bucks to get the shoe fixed. In the meantime, the amputated inflatable looked more than a bit odd. So what did the company do? It worked with a radio station and offered a reward for the return of the shoe. The station's morning talk-show hosts actually broadcast their show from the billboard site, waving to drivers as they passed by. Soon everyone was talking about the sign, the campaign, the newspaper, and the radio station. (By the way, the shoe was never returned and no one cared—the ad campaign worked with a great deal of resourcefulness.)

In this case, the theft of the shoe wasn't planned, but the lesson was pure Fields: Make the unexpected, or even the disastrous, work for you.

EXAMPLE 3: *Stammer in the court!* Now here's a real-life example of Fields-like resourcefulness. Sometimes a perceived liability can be an asset. A while back Shaun reported on a murder trial that pitted a green—and evidently stammering—young defense attorney against a loquacious prosecutor whose oratorical skills had previously carried him to the state governorship. Throughout the trial the ex-governor thundered, using every rhetorical device known to humankind. He had the jury and courtroom spectators spellbound as he built his case against the defendant. Both the press and the public were convinced that a quick conviction would result, particularly given the inexperience and the apparently impeded speech of the defense attorney. Not so! In fact, the stammering forced the jury to hang onto every word of the defense. Watching from the press table, one could see jurors' lips move as they completed the defense attorney's sentences, helping him along, bonding with him as he made the case against conviction. Interestingly enough, when the ex-governor was speaking, people smiled a lot, caught up in the music, the rhythms, the show—but they missed entirely the prosecutor's words, his argument, and the points of the evidence he stacked against the defendant. In the end, the defense attorney won. In a press interview after the trial, his stammer seemed to have been miraculously cured. W. C. would have loved it!

So be resourceful. Look for what can go wrong, be quick on your feet, and make lemonade from those lemons (or make twists for your martinis).

W. C.'S GUIDE TO RESOURCEFULNESS

When it comes to resourcefulness, W. C. demonstrates the power of four basic skills:

- The Power of Planning (Prepare for the things that can go wrong!)
- The Power of Change (Silence was golden, but the "talkies" were platinum!)
- The Power of Spontaneity (Never stick to a bad script!)
- The Power of Lemons (Think of a good twist when faced with a sour situation!)

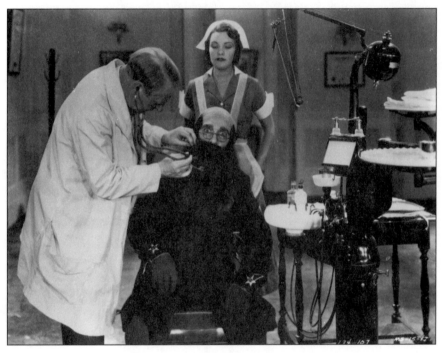

"Say, Ah . . . yes!" Even if you're a dentist, you may need to use creative ways just to find a patient's teeth. This is from the Mack Sennet short called The Dentist.

CHAPTER THREE

CREATIVITY AND INNOVATION

NECESSITY MAY BE THE MOTHER OF INVENTION, but in Fields's case, his mother was the inventor of his comedy and his father was the mother of his inventiveness. William Claude Dukenfield's mother inspired her son's sense of humor and his peculiar mumbling delivery of asides that W. C. Fields carried with him throughout his life. His father, on the other hand, unintentionally fostered Fields's creativity. "Pop" adamantly opposed his son's interest in juggling and refused to encourage it. Fields credited that lack of support for his success as a juggler.

"If he had given me money to learn and to buy tricks I would have purchased a whole act, and would have had nothing original," Fields said in later years. "He would not give me a cent, so I had to invent my own act and devise my own tricks."

Fields's creativity wasn't limited to juggling tricks, scripts, and roles. He developed a talent for drawing caricatures of his fellow vaudevillians that showed such professionalism he often sold these drawings to the local newspapers that advertised his traveling show. Furthermore, had he been less successful on the stage, he might well have become famous as an inventor. So instead of hawking his Yackwee Indian Medical Discovery and Pine Tar Remedy, a miracle cure for hoarseness, in a movie, he could have been the early 1900's Ron Popeil, of Ronco fame, pushing "Spray on Hair" in some sort of infomercial. Some of W. C.'s inventions were practical; most were mere comic fantasies, used as laugh getters in his movies. But they all worked for his purposes. Here are just a few, along with some practical lessons on how you can make your own ideas pay off:

- A practical napkin holder. (W. C. was very serious about this one.) Imagine a four-legged, four-inch high step stool. Now turn it upside down! Viola! You now have the W. C. Fields's napkin holder. He actually patented the idea. Make sure your brilliant idea works, and if it works, make sure it's wanted. If it's not, you'll end up like Fields with a garage full of napkin holders with no one to sell them to.

- The Necktie Soup Set (it contained six ties that matched in color and design the types of soup that might be spilled on them). In this decade, you might want to style it in various colors of brown to match the 50 different coffees you can get at Starbuck's. Same concept, different generation! Make your invention relevant to today's buyers.

- A trick table for billiard tricks (the table had a special rail that enabled balls to sail upward and back to the cue-wielder—W. C.—who would then catch them in his pocket or under his chin). The table also had hollow legs (as did Fields!). Fields actually drilled holes in the table and covered them with pasted velvet so he could pretend to jam his cue through hard slate for comic effect. The best ideas often spring from your need to solve a problem or perform a difficult task. When you learn to fully develop these fledgling concepts, you'll become known as a "problem solver" and an "idea person."

- A pogo-stick cocktail shaker (seen in *The Pharmacist*), enabling a child to burn off energy while generating a nerve-soothing drink for the old man. This particular invention failed to capture big-time sales because W. C. forgot to add a side container for olives. (A design flaw!) This is a perfect example of the need to think your brilliant idea all the way through.

- In *You're Telling Me*, Fields plays Samuel Bisbee, an inventor with a plethora of gadgets, including a keyhole funnel whose wide top helps navigate a key into a keyhole through the narrower bottom end. (This comes in particularly handy when one suffers the temporary lack of agility after an evening of Too Much Fun.)

  Bisbee has also created a burglar-catcher chair. He explains how it works to a couple of his bibulous friends as they drink lunch. "A thief comes into your house. You get friendly with him; offer him a drink. You lead him to this chair. When he sits down, this steel ball comes up and cracks him on the sconce, thusly." Sam demonstrates by putting his foot on the chair, and as advertised the steel ball flies up from behind the chair, "killing him immediately." The scene continues while

Sam swills a few, and then he finally, inadvertently, sits on his own "burglar-catcher chair." The iron ball knocks him into next year's cubicle design. His buddies continue killing the jug of swill, paying no mind to their evidently dead friend. After a while Bisbee wakes with a dull groan, looks at the ball, and shudders. Good news—he's not dead! Bad news—he's not dead. He studies the chair. Another design flaw! "Hmm, needs more work." This shows the need to thoroughly test your ideas to see if they actually do what they're supposed to do—without killing yourself.

Fields's inventiveness did not stop with gadgets; it continued into the realm of language and phraseology. Inspired by Dickens, he delighted in coining unusual names for people, places, and things: Gaboonport, Wisconsin; Cow Catcher, New Mexico; Schmackpfeiffer's Cruller Works; Colonel Catnip's Cat and Dog Circus; Mr. Whalebait; Prince Ranje Manje of Umbay; Hookallockah Meshobbab; J. Farnsworth Wallaby; A. Pismo Clam; Mrs. Hermosillo Brunch; Loudmouth McNasty; Eustace F. McGargle, F.A.S.N. (no one knows what the initials were supposed to stand for). Common phrases such as "a bat out of hell" became "a bat from the habitat of Old Ned."

To fuel his creativity he kept a dictionary on hand at all times and read it diligently looking for unusual words to incorporate into his scripts—words like "jabbernowl" (for nincompoop), "proboscis" (for his nose), and "what a euphonious appellation," which he says in *My Little Chickadee* when Mae West's character, Flower Belle Lee, tells his character, Cuthbert J. Twillie, her name. The words mean "nice-sounding name."

Developing your creative skills and those of others in your company can help give you a leg up on your competition. While some aspects of creativity seem innate, most can be learned. We've never met a "noncreative" person who wasn't far more creative than he or she realized after working at it.

At the end of this chapter we've summarized Fields's creative exercises, although he probably didn't know he was exercising. When you apply them, you'll find that you can emulate many of his constructions. But we'd also like to share with you tips from other experts on expanding your creative powers so you can come up with better ideas, boost your career, and help your company prosper.

When individuals work alone, they can be very creative, but when they work together and share ideas they can be even more creative. Loren Ankarlo and other consultants often use group creativity exercises to demonstrate the value of teamwork. In these exercises, the group will be presented with a common item, for example, a pencil, a paper clip, a Styrofoam cup, or a spoon. Then each person in a group will be asked to list as many uses as they can think of on a piece of paper. After five minutes, a show of hands is used to see who listed the most uses. (When we saw this done using a Styrofoam cup the top number of uses conceived by an individual was ten—some people came up with only 2 or 3.) Then the individuals are formed into small groups and asked to combine their lists, eliminating duplicate uses, and then work together to add to the list. They are again given about ten minutes. The results are astounding: Instead of one very creative person coming up with ten ideas, the group comes up with 15, 20, or—in the case we witnessed—more than 30!

Of course, one third of those ideas included various liquids you could put inside the cup and those were disqualified. None of the ten fluids, including pineapple juice, were allowed at work.

The more information, ideas, images, and experience you can draw on, the more fodder you have to fuel your creativity. Fields keenly observed the people and the activities around him and he fueled his mind with something more substantive than martinis—remember, he kept that dictionary at hand and read Dickens. You can learn a lot following his lead. Routine is the abyss into which creativity drops as we grow older. To keep sharp you need to vary your routines from time to time. Here are some things you might want to try.

Switch hands. If you're left-handed, try doing things with your right hand; if you're right-handed, try doing things with your left. (If you're ambidextrous, use your feet.) You're probably familiar with all of that "right-brain/left-brain" stuff so you know that the right side of the brain generally controls the left side of the body and vice versa. You also know that the right brain is credited with creative processes. We know one person who, when she is in a brainstorming session, always holds her pencil in her left hand even though she's right-handed. She also rotates her left foot and makes other small movements designed to work the left side of her body in order to stimulate the right side of her brain. By using these techniques, she finds her creative self works at top speed, but, on the downside, she can't read her notes once the meeting adjourns. In budget meetings, she favors the right side of her body, to stimulate the "logic" of her left brain. She says it helps her match her thinking style to the needs of the discussion. In order to stimulate creativity we suggest you use your left hand to light your cigar and hold

your martini glass. Then stand on your right leg while wearing a Vikings horned helmet, and singing *I'd Rather Have Two
Girls at Twenty-one Each Than One Girl at Forty-two.* If this
doesn't exactly stimulate creative thought, it will certainly
instill awe in your fellow workers.

Take up a new mental pursuit at least once a year. Learn a foreign language. Take up bird watching. Master a video game.
If you play chess, try the oriental game Go. If you play poker,
try bridge or chess. If you drink martinis, switch to Mai Tais.
At the end of the year, switch back. Whatever it is, work at it.

Move up a level in your normal pursuits. Many people work the
daily crossword puzzles in their newspapers long after they've
become easy. If you're still having trouble getting through
your current puzzles, stick with it; but, if it's become a piece
of cake, it's time to find a new puzzle. If you are easily com-
pleting most standard-style crosswords, take up diagramless
or cryptic crosswords. Whatever your daily pursuit, if it's
becoming too easy, it's time to move up a notch. Stretch that
brain! If you play Ping-Pong, switch to beanbag tossing. But
be careful. W. C. once attended the beanbag championship in
Paris. "Many people were killed!" according to him.

Keep notes or a diary of things that capture your attention. If
you're reading a book and like a quotation in it, don't just
dog-ear the page, write it down. If you see a painting you like,
make a note of who painted it, when it was painted, where
you saw it, and its medium. (Well, if it's medium, why are you
making such a fuss over it?) Like that wine? Make a note of it.
Do this after the first sip (if you wait to finish the bottle, you'll
never remember what you drank). When you write these
things down, you further embed them in your memory, where
you can draw on them to build creative ideas and expressions.

Fields, by the way, did this throughout his life. Whenever he got an idea—and he got lots of them—he wrote it down so it wouldn't be forgotten. Later he would reconsider the idea, discarding it or developing it until he had something that would work. Also, when he studied the dictionary and found a multisyllabic word that sounded like fun to him, he wrote the word down, copied its definition, and then wrote a sentence using the word.

A final note on creativity: Never waste an idea. W. C. didn't. If an idea failed the practical test as a real invention, he would incorporate it into his comedy routines or use it as a foil in his essays. That's how we know about the pogo stick cocktail shaker, the keyhole funnel, and the burglar-catcher chair. An idea that may be unworkable or seem silly as a "real" idea may still be useful in adding a bit of humor or as an anecdote in a corporate report or at a meeting.

Why all this attention to creativity? Because the workplace constantly needs creative solutions to boring problems, and if you're one of the problem solvers you will bring more money and productivity to the company, which we all know helps when promotion time rolls around. And now for some lessons from the man with the "roseate proboscis."

THE CREATIVE EXERCISES OF W. C. FIELDS

1. When you hear a cliché, think of new ways of saying the same thing. Substitute synonyms or a short definition for the key words in the old saw. Using this technique "a bat out of hell" might become "a winged mammal from Lucifer's lair," "between a rock and a hard place" might become "a mass of mineral material and a location unyielding to the touch." You get the idea. "What a euphonious appellation." (By the way, this also makes a semi-great party game!)

2. Think like the Dickens (Charles Dickens). Dickens was W. C.'s inspiration for using funny names in his films. He noted that Dickens did two things when creating names: He tied characteristics of a person to a name or to a sound (nasty sounds to nasty people, such as "Fagan" and "Scrooge," and trait-based names such as Gradgrind and McChokumchild to soul-deadening schoolmasters). Fields created characters named Repulsive Rogan and Loudmouth McNasty. He combined two common words to make an uncommon one (Dickens did it with "Copper" and "field"; Dickens also combined "magpie" and "witch" to create "Magwitch," and with a slight modification "fuzzy" and "wig" to create "Fezziwig." Fields did it with "pretty" and then he used his first name, William, or Willie to create "Prettywillie" (think about it!). Take unusual words that aren't names and make them names. Fields did it with Mrs. Hemoglobin and Mrs. Hermosillo Brunch. (Different from Dickens and Fields, however, you must keep your pet names private or you might find yourself calling your business manager Mr. Tightwad.)

3. Take note of recurring minor irritations, such as soup on your tie, and think of as many ways as possible to solve the problems they cause. That was no doubt the inspiration for the Necktie Soup Set and the keyhole funnel. For example, how many ways can you think of to retrieve your food when you wind up too far from the drive-up window at a fast-food chain? What kind of zipper would always rezip itself if you forgot? What kind of contraption would make sure you could always find your glasses in the morning? What kind of electronic gizmo would make sure your socks match? What about a self-lighting cigar? Again, these things won't boost sales, but like all exercise, it does tone the right side of your brain.

These are the types of exercises that kept Fields inventive throughout his life—and they're fun, to boot!

In any business you often are asked to wear many hats. In the Larsen E. Whipsnade business, a circus,
Fields as Whipsnade not only must wear many hats, he needs to wear many wigs and dresses, too.
But he manages all manner of change with aplomb.

C H A P T E R   F O U R

MANAGING CHANGE

W. C. WAS A MASTER OF CHANGE—HE HAD TO be. His lifetime spanned a period of massive transitions in the entertainment business— from vaudeville and Broadway revues, through the rise of motion pictures (and the change from silent to sound films), to the advent of radio. Fields also lived in a period of unprecedented social change: two world wars, the material wealth of the Roaring Twenties, the poverty of the Depression, the rise of the automobile. He witnessed the birth of commercial air traffic, Roosevelt's New Deal, Einstein's relativity, and Freud's psychology. When Fields was born, there were no telephones, cars, or record players; by the time he died, virtually every American household had one of each.

Fields had to continually change his act to respond both to social change and the change in media, and he did it all successfully while watching many of his vaudeville and silent-film partners sink into oblivion. Through it all, W. C. maintained his edge with techniques that are as applicable today as they were during Fields's lifetime.

Here are some thoughts on three basic types of change, with examples of how they apply in business and how W. C. handled them.

ORDINARY CHANGE

Ordinary change involves situations in which those making the change can control most of the variables. In business, this might involve extending a product into a new territory. The product is the same and the techniques of introducing it are likely the ones that have worked in previous introductions—only the geography and the vendors are different. The same is true for opening a new office: It's in a new location with new people, but the office will perform functions similar to those in other locations—as with a branch bank.

For W. C., ordinary change was as simple as moving from one stage to another—different night, different audience, same routine. Somewhat more complex, but still ordinary, would have been his transition from his silent juggling act on stage to a silent juggling act on film. Same act, different hours. Or the switch from vodka to gin. Same results, different elixirs. Most people are comfortable—even delighted—with ordinary change because they know what they're doing and their mission is clear.

By the way, one of the first changes Fields made was to change his name. He was born William Claude Dukenfield, but he clipped it to Field so it could appear in larger type. Later he changed it again. "I could never get managers to bill me as 'Field,' he once wrote. "They invariably added an 's.' I grew tired of remonstrating with them and added the 's.'" The name change may also have helped him get bookings. There were at least half a dozen popular vaudeville acts featuring people named Fields, and as a relative newcomer, W. C. no doubt benefited occasionally from mistaken association with their successes. Smart move, all around!

TRANSITIONAL CHANGE

Transitional change is another matter. It's required because business as usual isn't working. Perhaps a new competitor has moved into your market; demand for your product may be in a slow decline; you may no longer be able to attract the best and brightest people to your workforce; you may have found that your pricing structure is being undercut by more efficient operators. Everyone knows that something different must happen, that many things must change, but they also have a pretty clear idea of what must change.

Fields's career is rife with transitional change. For example, when silent films came along, vaudeville audiences started to decline. Fields recognized that he needed to reposition himself for the new industry and to devote more time to getting film work than stage work. His act didn't change, but his approach to landing contracts did.

His transition from stage to film positioned W. C. for his later transition from the silents to "talkies," whose appeal further weakened vaudeville. When "talkies" came along, Fields had two advantages many of his colleagues and competitors did not have: He had a distinctive voice, and he'd already familiarized himself with the motion-picture-making process. But the talkies also required W. C. to transition out of his old act away from the "tramp–juggler" character that had brought him to stardom. If he were to continue to grow in the entertainment industry, he had to remake himself to meet the needs of the talking screen. And he did.

The need for W. C. to change his act arose as much by age as by attitude. In 1915 Fields hit his 35th birthday and he realized that age had begun to cut the edge off his fabulous sharp juggling act, even if no one else noticed. As for attitude, Florence Ziegfeld signed the comic juggler to the Follies with a contract that made W. C. the highest paid juggler in history. He explained to his sister Adele why he decided to make a transitional change. He wrote that he had reached the top of his profession and had nothing more to prove—attitude; and he implied that he knew he could not juggle forever—age. So time and attitude forced him to decide to try something new. He would become a full-time comedian. He cut his juggling down to near nothing, wrote complete comedic skits, and remade himself into the Follies' top comedian. Fifteen years later, circumstances forced Fields into another transitional change. The Great Depression and talking films allied to dim the lights of Broadway and kill silent films. Fields had to pack his bags and move to Hollywood if he wanted to stay alive as an entertainer. This remains a transitional change and not a wholesale reversal or a long term change because, for the most part, Fields simply put his well-honed stage routines on film. Different times required different skills, a lesson that was not lost on Fields nor on the less adaptable stage and silent stars who fell into oblivion as the talkies and radio rose to dominance.

By making the transition from silent to sound films, Fields had also positioned himself for radio work. The voice, which he did not use early in his youth, now became his greatest asset in a medium where no one could see him or his old sight gags.

Throughout his career, Fields made continual, transitional change, each time setting up future opportunities. The lesson is clear: Transitions you make today position you for further adaptation—and growth—in the future. If Fields had not changed, he'd be about as famous today as Ben Blue, one of the hottest comedians of his day, but certainly not of ours.

LONG-TERM CHANGE

This is a capital "C" Change. It's needed when you or your company know that something's happening out there, but it is not yet possible to see clearly what your future state ought to be.

Fields's career, taken as a whole, illustrates the nature of long-term change. It's an ongoing process where ordinary change in the short term positions one for transitional change in the medium term and leads to something positive in the long term that could not have been predicted from the beginning.

W. C. entered show biz just before the turn of the century. Motion pictures had been invented, but they weren't yet an industry, and there was no Hollywood. While, in 1898, the young Fields certainly envisioned himself as a future star in vaudeville, he knew his long-term mission was to be funny and to attract the biggest audience possible. However, he could not have possibly imagined that he'd someday get top billing in a talking motion picture featuring an all-star cast of American and British actors, most of whom hadn't yet been born. But, in *David Copperfield,* he did just that. He certainly couldn't have imagined that he'd develop a screen and radio persona that involved an enlarged nose and voice gags (he was still a silent juggler, remember) or that the new media would enable him to be seen or heard by thousands, even millions, of people on a given night. The young Fields no doubt dreamed of fame, but it was his willingness to change, strive, and evolve that let him fulfill that dream. Unlike his character, Mr. Micawber in *David Copperfield,* W. C. did not just wait for "something to turn up." Instead, he changed to meet each turn!

CHANGING A TIRE COMPANY

The lives of companies often emulate the lives of individuals. If, 30 years ago, you'd asked someone at B. F. Goodrich what their company would be like today, you'd have gotten answers such as these:

- Short-term forecasters would have said, "We'll be selling more tires, and better tires, in more places, with better profits, than we are today."

- Transitionalists might have said, "We'll be selling more tires, and better tires, in more places, with better profits, than we are today—and we'll be expanding into other rubber-based, synthetic rubber-based and automotive after-market goods and services—all with better profit because of improvements in our operating processes."

- Long-term prognosticators might been thinking, "Maybe we'll be out of the tire business altogether. Should tires be what we are really all about? Is it a business of the future? What kinds of things should we be paying attention to in terms of foreign competition, consumer liability laws, and the industries of the future? As we develop and cash in on this mature industry we are in, should we be looking at growth industries of the future? What skills do we have in making tires that might be applied to other products?"

Today, of course, you can still buy B. F. Goodrich tires, but B. F. Goodrich doesn't make them. They left the tire business in 1986. Goodrich tires now are made and marketed by Michelin. Today's B. F. Goodrich describes itself this way:

"The B. F. Goodrich Company provides aircraft systems and services and manufactures performance materials. The company's strengths in technology and research enable the rapid development and commercialization of new products and allow us to give our customers a competitive edge."

Recognizing that its core strength was not "making tires" but rather its knowledge of synthetics, the company today has a Performance Materials division that is, arguably, the leading global producer of performance polymer systems and additives that include textile coatings, finishing chemicals, colorants and pigments; coatings and emulsions for paper, wood, and metal; additives for adhesives, water treatment, lubricants, and rubber; thickeners, film formers and colorants for personal care, home care, and industrial products; ingredients for food and beverage; active and inactive ingredients for pharmaceuticals; and specialty plastics (Goodrich scientists did, after all, invent synthetic rubber!).

During its years as a tire company, Goodrich successfully landed many large-scale military and civilian contracts and developed experience as an automobile service company through its many sales and service outlets. Recognizing that its skills in bidding and service could be leveraged, it put its knowledge to use. Today BFGoodrich Aerospace provides advanced systems, products, and services. Virtually every aircraft flying in the world today is or can be equipped or serviced by BFG Aerospace. Representative products of BFGoodrich Aerospace include aircraft engine nacelles, pylons, and thrust reversers; wheels, brakes, and landing gear; emergency evacuation systems; sensors; ice protection systems; instruments and avionics; collision warning and storm detection systems; and flight management and control systems. Significantly, the company is also North America's largest independent third-party provider of maintenance, repair, and overhaul services to major airlines worldwide.

Once it stopped being "tired" and transformed itself into a technology company, Goodrich's worldview changed, too. While its divisions are still headquartered in Ohio, it now considers itself a global company, serving global markets and maintaining operations located in 11 nations. That's transformational change. And it resulted from an assessment of the company's core strengths, not its traditional products. It came step by step, each incremental and transitional change setting the change for the transformation.

Today, B. F. Goodrich is a remarkably successful company. Between 1993 and 1998 its sales grew by more than 50 percent, its operating profits more than doubled, and its profits from ongoing business more than tripled. No one doubts that, had it stayed in the tire business, its numbers wouldn't be that good.

By the way, we like the Goodrich example because Fields once played an inventor—Sam Bisbee in *You're Telling Me*—whose greatest invention (besides his burglar-catcher chair) was a puncture-proof tire. Eventually, he sells the patents to a fictional tire company. Today puncture-proof tires are widely advertised, but not made by Goodrich, which decided that its duty to its shareholders was better served by building a puncture-proof company.

John Scherer is a veteran consultant who specializes in helping business leaders transform their lives and their organizations. In his presentations, Scherer tells his audiences that "there is a correct or appropriate time and place for each type of change" and warns that "if you approach a situation in the wrong change mode, it can often blow up in your face, or maybe even worse, simply die with a whimper, causing you to slide back into the morass of the past or old way of doing things."

Neither Fields nor Goodrich has let that happen—and you can't afford to either.

W. C.'S GUIDE TO CHANGE

- Silence may be golden, to a silent juggler, but when it's time to talk you have to speak up!
- One good change deserves another, and another, and another . . .
- Sometimes you have to stop juggling and begin to annunciate.
- Change is the path to success. It's also good for vending machines!
- Changing your name may help; but changing your act is essential.

If the ball lands in your "court," trust your fellow associate to dislodge it. In this case Fields plays Ping-Pong actively utilizing a "team effort" concept allowing uninterrupted play.

CHAPTER FIVE

MAKING
TEAMWORK WORK

"I AM READY TO TAKE UP ARMS AT A MOMENT'S NOTICE. THE LEGS WE CAN TAKE UP LATER." THE MAKING OF A MOVIE IS THE ULTIMATE TEAM effort, and it usually involves a team of high-powered, Type-A personalities: the producer, the director, the stars, the writers, all of their agents, investors, and expert technicians whose egos often surpass those of the people for whom they work. The team must deal with the temperaments of cast and crew, and must do so under the extreme pressure of shooting schedules. Once the shooting itself is done, the film moves to the hands of additional teams made up of composers, musicians, editors, and post-production crews. The end product of the team effort must appear seamless to moviegoers. Any behind-the-scenes tensions must be invisible when the film hits the screens—and they usually are.

How does Hollywood, known for having thousands of egos bigger than W. C. Fields's proboscis, routinely produce teams that produce successful multimillion-dollar projects that enthrall filmgoers worldwide? What does Hollywood know about teams that other businesses can learn from? Fields's career gives us some insights.

W. C. often found himself in movies with other great talents—Burns and Allen, Bob Hope, Ben Blue, Edgar Bergen, and Mae West among others. When he had to appear with them, each celebrity was rightfully concerned that he or she receive fair billing in the credits and a fair share of screen time. Each performer needed a chance to show off his or her routines, connect with his or her fans, and generate plenty of laughs. If they didn't fight for their due, you can bet their agents fought for them.

Ideally, by the time a movie hits production-ready status, several key factors ensuring good teamwork will be in place.

1. The mission is clear. The team is going to make a specific movie, using a specific script that each team member has read.

2. Each team member knows what his or her role will be. Each person knows what lines he or she will deliver, what scenes he or she will appear in, and with whom he or she will appear, scene by scene.

3. Everyone knows how his or her contribution will be credited. In some cases, the cast is listed in order of appearance; in others, the cast hierarchy will be determined either by the size of the role or the size of the star. (For instance, in *David Copperfield*—arguably Fields's greatest triumph—W. C. worked for only ten days playing a semi-minor character, Wilkins Micawber. Nevertheless, his star status secured him top billing in the movie, ahead of such greats as Lionel Barrymore, Maureen O'Hara, Basil Rathbone, and Roland Young.)

4. Team members know the terms of their compensation and the benefit they will derive if the movie is a hit. (Compensation for a hit varies. The stars, director, producers, and executive producers will usually share in the profits of the film, over and above their salaries. For others the advancement of their career and promotion up the cast list and money list the next time around creates a tremendous incentive to do their best, even though they will not receive immediate financial remuneration. Hollywood works much as the business world does in that regard.)

5. All team members know that when the movie is over, the team—having accomplished its mission—will be reconfigured: The stars will move on to other team efforts with other co-stars; the director will start a new movie, often with a different producer. The next project will involve different stunt persons, different caterers, different makeup crews, different camera personnel. This means that a film team's mission is limited in time. No matter what conflicts occur, most will be short-lived (although sometimes they can haunt—even kill—careers). In most, but certainly not all films, everyone tries to keep an outward appearance of cooperation and help. They try to pretend that this "team" will stay together forever. Why? Because Los Angeles is a huge city, but the film community is a small town. Many of the team members they work with today, they will see again on other films. If you're good some of them may even help advance your career . . . not unlike team play in corporate America. The world may laugh about phony Hollywood, but these people know well never to take artistic differences per-

sonally. You may hate someone today, but tomorrow you may need to work with that person. Hollywood has taught us to express differences, but to keep it on a professional level. In short, hide all ill will!

Put these five factors in place and you've laid the groundwork for any successful team effort. Leave any one of them out and your team will likely fail to produce the results you need, not least because the team members are likely to wind up at each other's throats. The bottom line: Teamwork works when the goals are as clear as the nose on W. C.'s face.

My Little Chickadee provides a perfect example of the catastrophes that can occur when the Five Rules for Successful Teams are ignored. The movie stars Fields and Mae West were two people who were notorious for the demands they made on directors and scriptwriters. Neither was a shrinking violet and both delighted in ad-libs, gibes, and scene-stealing, which means they didn't let everyone know the script. West's and Fields's approach to *Chickadee* muddied the waters of teamwork. The mission was unclear, the roles were ill-defined, and only they knew how the final script would read. In other words, they trampled on the first three rules for successful teams.

(Humphrey Bogart had a chance to play a big role in *Chickadee* and was excited about sharing the screen with Fields and West. Then he read the script. The first five pages read just fine, but on the sixth page he read a simple note: "The next ten pages to be supplied by W. C. Fields." He read the next five pages, which were followed by another note: "The next ten pages to be supplied by Mae West." These his-and-her sections alternated throughout the incomplete script. Bogey smelled trouble and turned down the part.)

Ironically, the West–Fields relationship had started off as an alliance. Preproduction letters between them dealt with problems they had had with directors, the studio, script changes, and the like. All was very cordial as they joined forces against everyone else. They may have thought that was good for "their team," but it certainly wasn't good for the team as a whole. The Fields–West pact was the Hollywood equivalent of the early alliance between Hitler and Stalin during World War II. And like the dictators, once W. C. and Mae had achieved their initial goals together, they started going after each other. When the cameras began cranking on *My Little Chickadee,* their war began cranking, too.

Sometimes Fields went on the attack, even before the director ordered "Action!" Right before one scene, Fields turned to a crony and within earshot of Ms. West intoned, "Ah, yes, there's Mae West, a fine figure eight of a woman . . . and so well preserved." Another time he told a visiting reporter—moments before the cameras rolled and again within earshot of West—"Oh look, there's Mae West! She's a plumber's idea of Cleopatra." Action! Not a pleasant way for her to begin a scene.

(Fields's team-destroying antics certainly left a lasting impression. Thirty years after the release of *My Little Chickadee,* I was scheduled to appear on a talk show and the producer asked if I would mind sharing an interview with Mae West. I told him I would be honored. When I arrived at the studio, however, Mae was a no-show. When I asked the producer why, he said that Ms. West told him, "I don't want to meet another Fields as long as I live!")

My Little Chickadee was a box-office success, but a critical failure when it was released. Today, however, the film is considered a comedy classic, despite the failure of teamwork on its set. For all their bickering on the sound stage, the greatness of Fields and West shone through in their individual scenes. *My Little Chickadee* is not a good film, but the great parts have enabled the whole to survive. (Indeed, the famous pose adorning the cover of this book hails from *Chickadee*.) Only high-caliber talents such as Fields and West could have pulled success from the ashes of failed teamwork that marked *My Little Chickadee*. Even with extraordinary talent, the odds are against you if your team doesn't come together.

While Fields and West did not make a successful team, they did make a successful film. And their differences illustrate an important aspect of teamwork: Teamwork does not require friendship. Team members don't have to like each other. Rodgers and Hammerstein didn't. Gilbert and Sullivan didn't. The great New York Yankee teams of the 1950s and '60s certainly didn't. But there are very rare exceptions.

Team members have to be able to rely on each other within the context of the team's mission. They must know what to expect from other members of the team. They must, above all, respect their teammates' talents, even if they are jealous of those talents. Not only are you not required to like your teammates, you don't even have to get along with them all of the time, but it certainly helps. Accept—even welcome—differences of opinion. We've seen many teams formed in which people fail to passionately state their positions on issues, for fear of destroying the team process. When that happens, teams fail because ideas are not adequately tested before they are launched. Getting along becomes more important than reaching your goal and getting the right thing done.

Having trampled on the rules that govern good teams, Fields and West couldn't get beyond the turmoil.

Consequently, with *My Little Chickadee* the original goal of making a great film was not met. The bottom line: When putting together a team, try to stock it with people who can work and play well with others. If you don't have that option, make sure the ground rules are clear. Then you can produce not only great scenes, but a great film, as well.

In one scene in *The Bank Dick*, Egbert Sousé's future son-in-law, Og Oggilby, turns to Fields and says, "I was a perfect fool to listen to you!"

W. C. responds, "You listen to me, Og, nothing in this world is perfect!"

Good teamwork won't create perfection, but it will create improvement and the possibility of continuous improvement.

FIVE RULES FOR SUCCESSFUL TEAMS

- Make the mission clear.
- Make the roles clear.
- Make everyone read and know the "script."
- Make the rewards clear.
- Make the timeframe clear and as short as possible.

Looks like the President of Klopstokia, W. C. Fields, could use the lessons in our next chapter, Delegation.

CHAPTER SIX

DELEGATION

"DON'T DO
WHAT I
TOLD YOU
TO DO, DO
WHAT I
TELL YA!"

IN *You Can't Cheat an Honest Man*, Fields plays Larsen E. Whipsnade (don't miss the Larsen E.), the owner and manager of a circus that traipses from county to county just a subpoena-length ahead of the law and a cabal of creditors. Near the end of the film, and with his circus barely above the sawdust, we find Larsen E. running late for his beloved daughter's wedding at the posh home of the socially elite Bel-Goodies. "Ah, yes, they're the crème de la crème, the noblesse oblige. We've got acrobats in our circus."

Right before leaving his little enterprise, he applies the age-old adage, "The circus must go on," even as the wedding proceeds. Whipsnade must delegate. Ah, yes, but to whom should he entrust his empire? Which one of the nefarious conniving lot who work for him can he put in charge? He checks the prospects. His extremely dimwitted, noncommunicative assistant seems the perfect man. But he will first have to pass a test.

"On account of your unimpeachable integrity and business persicacity—you know what that is, don't you?"

The rube, wearing a baffled smile, shakes his head, replying in the negative.

"That's fine—why, because of that, I'm putting you in charge of the circus."

Perfect! Satisfied with the man's complete ignorance, W. C. puts him in charge, confident that his circus will be free of sabotage, and if the law or creditors mosey by they will get absolutely nowhere with this idiot.

The point: Delegating authority is not always a matter of finding the best person for the job, but rather finding the best person to do the job the way you want it done. Or as Fields might say, "Finding the one person who cannot devise perfidious designs on your position."

Although he delegates effectively (given the outcome he wants) in *You Can't Cheat an Honest Man*, W. C. was not a person who delegated much authority in real life. He believed his brand of comedy was unique and preferred to write, or substitute, his own lines instead of following the scripts prepared by other writers, whom he considered his comedic inferiors. (Fields used the example of a writing session at which a writer spewed out a line. W. C. told him that the line came directly out of Fields's last movie. The writer simply laughed and said he knew he stole it from somewhere, he just couldn't remember where.) Fields never delegated to an accountant, preferring to manage his own money. He had an inherent distrust of agents (indeed, all intermediaries) and abhorred the use of doubles in his film sequences. As the President of Klopstokia in the movie *Million Dollar Legs*,

W. C. portrays a chief executive who fails to delegate anything, not even a presidential fanfare. Instead, when he enters
a room he plays the fanfare himself on his strapped-on
portable orchestra complete with percussion, brass, and
strings. Indeed, in many ways, both on and off screen, Fields
was a one-man band.

But if you really want to delegate successfully no matter
how many books you read on the art of delegation, it all
comes down to five basic points:

1. Successful leaders and managers can get more things
   done faster and better when they work through other
   people and spread the load.

2. Make sure people know what the rules and tasks are
   before you ask them to do something for you.

3. Make sure the people whom you ask to do things are
   capable, trustworthy, and responsible.

4. Make sure the people you ask to do things, do the things
   you ask.

5. Be available to advise the people to whom you delegate.

DELEGATING BLAME

In the short-subject film *The Dentist*, Fields begins the piece
playing golf with his pal Frobisher. In a foul mood all morning, Fields and Frobisher along with their caddie finally arrive
at a tee whose green can be found in the middle of a duck-
filled pond. Fields drives the ball, and it lands in the drink. He
immediately delegates blame; it's the squawking ducks. He
tees up again and the ball finds water again. He delegates

blame; this time he finds the perfect foil—his caddy. "Don't stand over there, stand over here." The caddy obeys and moves to a spot behind Fields. The third ball misses land once again. Aha! The caddy! "Don't stand behind me when I'm shooting! Stand over there!" W. C. points to the very spot the caddy stood at the second shot. The caddy protests, "But you told me to stand here, sir." W. C. replies, "Never mind where I told you to stand. You stand where I tell you!" He mumbles a complaint to Frobisher, "He's so dumb, he probably doesn't even know what time it is."

Frobisher: "Say, what time is it?"

W. C.: "I don't know!"

Caddy: "It's ten-fifteen!"

W. C.: "Shut up!"

Fields takes a fourth shot and once again the ball makes a splash down. He waits a beat, then throws his club into the pond. Frobisher complains, "Oh wait! You can't do that!"

W. C.: "What do you mean I can't do that?" He grabs his stuffed golf bag and hurls that into the lake. "I can do anything I want to do." He then grabs the caddy by the nape of his neck and the back of his pants and throws him into the water. After all, it was his fault the shots went afoul in the first place.

Which brings us to the question of delegating blame: Don't do it! It nearly always backfires. A great deal of the humor in the scene on the golf course comes from the fact that we feel sympathy for the poor caddy. If an action by you or someone under you or above you creates a sudden "boon-doggle," concentrate on fixing the problem rather than on attaching blame. If you're in charge, just like a coach on an athletic team, you must take responsibility. If the guy above you made the mistake, look good by not pointing fingers but rather use your finger to plug the dike.

This golf course example raises another issue: In the course of delegating a task or responsibility, your directions must be as clear as an extra-dry gin martini. Communicate exactly what you want done; how, exactly, you want it done; and when, exactly, you need it done. It also helps to explain why you want it done. People like knowing how their work fits into the big picture, just as you do. If you have to alter direction in the middle of a project, give an explanation. In short, communicate! (Fields knew the importance of communication. Almost all of his humor revolves around misstatements and misunderstood comments. For a comedian who started out as a *silent* juggler, Fields turned out to be the most quotable and most verbal of all of the comedians of the "Golden Age of Comedy." In delegating blame to the caddie, Fields poked fun at the way we communicate delegation, "Never mind where I told you to stand. You stand where I tell you!" Fields does none of the things we suggested and that's why the routines bring laughs.)

THE JOY OF DELEGATION

There's an ironic aspect to delegation, and it's this: Many people who are very good at delegating in their personal lives are often poor delegators in the workplace. Here are three detailed examples, illustrating the ways good delegation can help make your life easier. These involve actual cases, but to protect the guilty we've replaced real names with fictitious names from Fields's movies:

1. *Expense control*

A. Pismo Clam manages four departments with 300 employees. Pismo prides himself on cost control and insists upon seeing every employee's monthly report for expense reimbursements. The reimbursements average about $100 and range in size from less than $10 to as much as $1,500. He meticulously goes over each report himself, which gives him little time to devote to other things. It's a big day for A. Pismo when he finds that Egbert Sousé in the Sales Department slipped in a "Health Bar" bill and seeks reimbursement for a double pineapple juice, a disallowed expense! Meanwhile, Mrs. Muckle, a major customer decides to cancel her account because Pismo hasn't had time to return her phone call.

Cost of losing the customer: A $50,000-a-year account!

Savings for catching the health bar nut: $3.25! Holy Clams!

If Pismo were an effective delegator, he would have first set out the rules for expense reimbursement and made sure a copy of the rules had reached each employee's hands. Then he would have trained his four department heads to review and approve the expenses of the people reporting to them. Pismo would have continued to review the expense reports of the four people answerable directly to him, but he would have made sure they handled everyone else. Pismo also should have reserved the right to sign off on all reimbursements that exceeded, say, $1,200. Or, he should have obtained monthly reports on total reimbursements. If the reports showed a problem, Pismo should have asked questions. If no questions were needed, then he should have been happy knowing his system worked.

2. Correspondence

Jaspar Fitchmueller works for a publishing company. "Fitch" liked to sort his own mail and e-mail and insisted on dictating all responses. He received routine e-mails and letters asking for permission to reprint material in the company's publications. The volume of these requests had escalated over the years, and Fitchmueller found himself spending nearly a third of his time dictating responses to his secretary, Cleopatra Pepperday. Fortunately, Ms. Pepperday understood delegation and gave Fitch some worthwhile advice.

"A lot of these letters are pretty much the same," she told him. "I've already developed e-forms for most of them. Why don't I take the letters and send out the responses, so you can do other things?" They spent four hours discussing the nature of requests they've received in the past and drafting standard letters of reply. From that point on, Cleopatra handled all the responses, saving both of them a lot of time. When a request came in that didn't fit the model replies created, Cleo brought the new request to Fitch and they considered the best way to handle it. Then they drafted a new form letter to cover that type of request in the future. Results: The requests were answered more quickly, sometimes by a simple keystroke, and Fitch and Cleopatra both have more time to perform other tasks. Once every quarter, Cleo provides Fitch with an interoffice e-mail summary report that shows the number of requests received, whether permission was granted or denied, and whether the conditions under which permission was granted have been met. The report enables Fitch to stay on top of the volume and nature of the requests. (By the way, Fitch and Cleo fell in love, got married, and created four e-mail children. Baffles science!)

3. Research

Cordelia Neselrode started her career as an assistant and specialized in research. Indeed, she'd risen in the company on the basis of her outstanding and well-documented reports. Neselrode could get more out of a library search in an hour than most people could get in a day. She was promoted and promoted until she had no more time to dig out research materials herself. Meetings, employee conferences, correspondence, phone calls, e-mails, and business travel replaced her solid research. Fortunately, she was able to coast on her reputation for a couple of years, but she knew that her reports were not what they used to be. That's when she decided to start delegating. Instead of taking an inadequate 30 minutes to do her own research, she spent 30 minutes meeting with her assistant, Farnsworth Wallaby. She told Farnsworth to pack up and head for the company's research center. She gave him specific directions, which she thought would help. The first time or two he handled a research project, Farnsworth came up short, finding only scanty or inapplicable types of information. Each time, Cordelia reviewed his procedures, reviewed her specifications, and shared suggestions on how Farnsworth might improve his findings. Eventually Neselrode learned how to give better specifications and Farnsworth learned how to do better searches. The result: Farnsworth now does all of the research and Cordelia has more facts—and lots more time in which to interpret them.

As the examples show, it takes time to put an effective system of delegation in place: time to train, time to set up the processes, time to find the right people, but it's time well spent. Any effective delegator will tell you that the time spent setting up the process has been quickly recovered and has produced returns beyond the dreams of temporal avarice.

W. C.'S GUIDE
TO DELEGATION

- Managers who say, "Don't do what I told you do, do what I tell ya!" usually get clubbed.
- Sometimes "the best person" for the job is not the obvious choice.
- The eleventh commandant is "Don't dawdle, delegate."
- Judge not the effectiveness of your delegatee before you've given him or her the tools and processes to do the job. Like in golf, a caddy cannot do his or her job properly if you don't tell the caddy where you keep the olives.
- Often, delegating means getting someone to perform a task you prefer not to perform and the delegatee doesn't have to perform. However, if the delegatee does it anyway, always remember the immortal words of W. C.: "Never smarten up a chump."

In order to budget properly, according to W. C., you need money. Here in Poppy Fields appears to have budgeted enough to give exact change to Lynne Overman who just bet on the shell game.

C H A P T E R   S E V E N

BUDGETING

W. C. FIELDS FIRST DESCRIBED HIS APPROACH TO budgeting in an article he intended for his 1941 classic book *Fields for President*, his platform for his spoof run at the White House. For reasons unknown, it never got into his book, but I published it in *W. C. Fields: By Himself.* In his essay, Fields gave us a perspicacious look at how he would eliminate waste in managing the government's budget.

In order to feed the government's ungainly bureaucracy, Fields proposed the "glass-jar" method of allocating the tax-payers' hard-earned cash and imparted his hypothesis to the rulers of our fair democracy. He also had a few "tall-tale" angles on the origins of budgeting, its applications, and the steps needed to balance a budget—including the ultimate step. We are reprinting the essay here in its entirety so you can enjoy Fields at his finest as a humorist and glean a full understanding as to why he was never considered CFO material.

HOW TO BEAT A BUDGET
By W. C. Fields

The last time Congress called me in to confer on the national budget, I became truly exasperated. "Gentlemen," I exploded, "how many times have I told you that you will never get anywhere in this matter until you purchase seven glass jars and label them (neatly!) UPKEEP, INTEREST ON DEBTS, RUNNING EXPENSES, SAVINGS, NATIONAL DEFENSE, SEEDS FOR CONSTITUENTS, and INCIDENTALS. If you distribute your tax intake into those jars each month, you will have the beginnings of a workable budget system—and not before!"

While the entire legislative body sat stunned under the sting of my words, I took my hat and stalked out, with the sergeant-at-arms behind me—and catching up with me, kindly urging me toward the door.

I suppose, my friends, that not one person out of a thousand knows that I am considered positively the *last* authority on budgeting. But it is true. Whenever any of my intimate companions have budget trouble, I am positively the last person they come to for advice. I attribute my deep understanding of the subject to my friendship with the late Orrin F. Budget from whose name the word derived.

Orrin used to own a bustling little saloon back in Gaboonport, Wisconsin. He was a turf-lover of the first water and owned, besides the barroom, an enviable string of racehorses. Among them were a stout stallion named Heat and Light, a dainty filly named Rent, a goodly bay gelding named

Food and Clothing, and several promising two-year-olds known as Insurance, Recreation and Incidentals.

Now it happened that I often dropped into Orrin's establishment for a handful of potato chips. One day I noticed Orrin at a corner table slipping bills into envelopes. He would place, say, four dollars in an envelope marked Rent, six dollars in an envelope marked Heat and Light, and so on. I asked him what he was doing.

"Oh," he stammered, "I—well, I'm just portioning out running expenses."

"I see," I said. "You mean you're Budgeting."

"I suppose you might call it that," he admitted.

Since that day, everyone *has* called it budgeting. And, gentle reader, in spite of the fact that he never won a bet on any of his horses, that first budget system of his, embryonic as it was, worked better than any I have ever known since. After all, he could never starve to death while his saloon served the excellent free lunch it did.

Ever since my association with Orrin F. Budget, I have been a rabid supporter of the planning economy for the family unit. Indeed, I resent slurs and petty jokes upon the budget as if they were reflections on my own honor, which I pride among all material things. Just the other evening, for instance, I attended a bank directors' dinner and the "learned" gentleman at my side made light of the budget. He said, "Show me a woman who keeps a budget and I'll show you a woman who's wearing a gas bill on her head." He said, further, that a young couple would be much better off to just put their money away and forget about it (until the bank fails, I thought).

Frankly, friends, I was enraged. "Faw!" I retorted witheringly, "if 'just putting money away' is such a fine cure-all, how do you explain this?" Then I cited the case of Young Wolfgang Brown and his bride. When they moved into their little apartment, they started "putting money away" faithfully. Each week they would take two-thirds of Wolfgang's salary and tuck it away in the corner of a little built-in cabinet. At the end of the first month, when the bills arrived, they went proudly to the cabinet for their savings. They found no money there. They couldn't even find any cabinet. For the first time they realized it was a dumbwaiter!

When challenged with this irrefutable argument, my dinner companion was "stymied." He turned the color of his tomato bisque and slipped quietly under the table. I did not follow him for another half-hour, but it certainly was a rousing Fields victory . . .

To be really successful, a budget should have a definite objective. By that I mean that the budgeter should have some inspiring ambition to spur him on in his great project. Take me, for instance, in the year 1909 (back in those days I was *worth* taking!). In the spring of 1909 I was just entering upon majority, and I had become enamoured of a certain Miss Renee de Bureaudraugh, a comely Titian belle with a small spread-eagle tattooed on her left shoulder blade.

Renee promised that she would marry me when I had saved $150.00. I was in eighth heaven, having ridden past my floor in ecstatic confusion. I immediately secured a job as clerk with E. G. Fernley, Inc., Haberdashers. My salary was $17.00 a week. With the picture of Renee always before my eyes (not to mention the spread-eagle) I sold shirts at a whirlwind pace. My first great triumph came when ex-President Hoover dropped into the store for a handkerchief. Before he could get out, I had sold him half a dozen soft collars!

E. G. Fernley himself wept on my shoulder with pride and promptly promoted me to manager. I was now earning $14.00 per week (times were bad). But E. G. Fernley himself helped me to rearrange my budget so that I would still be making progress in my campaign for Renee's hand. He advised me to cut out my after-dinner toothpick and to limit myself to one new pair of shoelaces per month: moreover, chewing gum was to have no place in my new scheme of things.

But at the end of four months I had only $2.34 in my savings account, and I was beginning to feel discouraged. However, I was soon to execute another coup d'etat, as the Russians have it. I put my managerial hand to work and invented a pair of shoes with rubbers painted on them, specially designed for husbands whose wives feel they cannot be trusted outdoors in damp weather.

These shoes sold like hotcakes, and E. G. Fernley himself fell on the floor in a paroxysm of joy. To reward me, he made me vice-president, at $11.00 per week. I was somewhat disappointed at the stipend, but he made up the discrepancy by rearranging my budget for me again: I was to give up squandering coins on subway scales, reduce my consumption of cigarette-lighter fluid and cut out dental floss all together.

In spite of my rapid progress in the business world, I seemed as far from winning my Renee as ever. But my spirit was not broken. One night I woke from a sound sleep and invented the Necktie Soup Set, which I have always considered one of the greatest contributions to American cleanliness. The set consisted of six neckties: a sea-green tie for split pea wear, a beige tie for chicken-gumbo wear, old-rose for cream of tomato and a lettered design for alphabet soup. The remaining two ties were of Scotch heather for utility wear.

The innovation literally saved the company from bankruptcy. Every man in town with a spark of neatness in his system rushed to the store to buy a set. E. G. Fernley was completely overcome with gratitude and forthwith resigned as president in my favor. I felt very proud of my newly won high position, but since it paid only $6.50 per week, I soon became uneasy. So uneasy, in fact, that I went to E. G. Fernley and asked if I could not have my old clerk's job back again.

"Will," he said, "if it were in my power to grant you that request, I would do so with all my heart. But the truth is that I've got the job now, and I simply can't afford to give it up."

"I understand," I murmured reverently. "But tell me, Mr. Fernley, how am I to manage on my budget?"

"Well, let us put our heads together on the problem," he comforted me.

We did, but we could not figure out one more item that I could economize on. Mr. Fernley did suggest that I give up the luxury of blowing the collar off my beer, but I felt that that was just too much. We were finally about to give up and admit defeat, when E. G. Fernley cried out, "Eureka!"

"What is it?" I gasped with baited breath.

"Something neither of us has ever thought of!" he howled exultantly. "And so simple, too. Will, all you have to do is cut out Miss Renee de Bureaudraugh!"

My throat choked up in admiration. "Mr. Fernley, I'll never be able to thank you for the help you've given me," I gulped.

There was a great mind, friends! I followed his advice and have never had a minute's worry since. I commend it to each and every one of you as a revolutionary development in the field of budgeting.

Well, my friends, I think that little interlude should prove to anyone what results can be had from a well-planned budget that is followed out faithfully.

If you have any further questions, write me a letter—but please enclose a stamped envelope. I'm using this month's Postage to play the Irish Sweepstakes.

BUDGETING BY FIELDS

As a budget adviser, Fields was clearly more Baron Munchhausen than Baron Rothschild, but having made a good living most of his adult life—at one time he was the sixth highest-paid person in America—he could juggle finances almost as well as he could juggle billiard balls. That's why he could be so funny when he wrote about money. And not only funny—but damned canny!

Reduced to its essence, here is the unarguable advice on budgeting contained in "How to Beat a Budget."

- All budgets have a goal.

- Budgets break down expenses into clearly defined categories.

- When budgeted revenue falls short, budgeted expenses must be reduced.

- If budgeted revenue cannot be recovered through expense cuts, the goal must be abandoned. (A company's desired bottom line frequently suffers the fate of Miss Renee de Bureaudraugh when revenues fall short!)

As to the "seven-jars" program, it, too, has some basis in good budget practice. For example:

- First, it is zero-based. Fields suggests that Congress start from scratch.

- Second, like any good budget system, the jars divide expenditures into meaningful categories (though W. C.'s *could* be a little more meaningful).

- Third, the jars separate fixed expenses (such as Running Expenses) from variable expenses (such as incidentals). That's really important.

Of course, seven jars aren't enough, and Fields's National Budget Plan deals only with expenses. He doesn't mention revenues. We get no clue how much money we're budgeting.

Also, in the "seven-jars" section he doesn't say what the budget's goal is (perhaps because audiences would assume that simply getting the federal budget in balance in 1939 would have been a victory).

Clearly Fields's proposed budget is a rolling budget, with each month's revenue allocated as it comes in, requiring adjustments on the fly to make sure that if some jars got too full they could feed the jars that always seemed empty.

Fields may have suggested the government use glass jars for budgeting because, like the federal budget, they could be so easily broken.

Budgeting, to adopt W. C.'s metaphor, requires you to know not only how many jars to use and what size they should be, but also how much you're going to put into each jar, how often you're going to put it in, and how much and how often you're going to take money out of the jars—or occasionally break one.

W. C. FIELDS,
CHIEF FINANCIAL OFFICER

- Get yourself seven jars. (Divide your expenses into meaningful categories, and if you can't find jars, use bottles, but make sure you empty them first.)

- When revenues fall, cut out chewing gum before you cut out dental floss. (Make healthful decisions.)

- When you can't make the budget, ask yourself: Do I really want Miss Renee de Bureaudraugh? (Revisit your objectives and see if they're realistic.)

- Separate variable and fixed expenses (and keep enough on hand for ol' Heat and Light in the eighth!).

- Watch those investments and deposits! Avoid sucker stocks, tulip bubbles, Ponzi schemes, uninsured banks, and, most of all, dumbwaiters!

Sometimes you must stand firm when negotiating as Fields and Allison Skipworth graphically indicate here.

C H A P T E R   E I G H T

THE ART OF NEGOTIATION

> **"I'D RATHER HAVE TWO GIRLS AT 21 EACH THAN ONE GIRL AT 42."**

FIELDS WAS A MASTER NEGOTIATOR BOTH ON AND off the screen. On screen he parades his skills at their sharpest in the 1934 film, *It's a Gift.* Fields, as Harold Bissonette, turns a worthless piece of land into a nifty orange grove through hard-nosed negotiating techniques.

Subscribing to the Fields's adage, "When there's a will . . . prosperity can't be far behind," Harold Bissonette, a New Jersey grocer, waits for his elderly Uncle Bean to die. Harold knows that when the terribly sad event occurs, he stands to inherit $5,000; enough money to cover the down payment on his dream California orange ranch.

One day at the grocery (after Harold reminds his assistant to "Never call me Mr. Bissonette in front of Mrs. Bissonette, it's Bisso-nay!"), Harold's wife, Amelia, enters the store with distressing news. Uncle Bean stands "at death's door!" Harold wonders, "Do you think they can pull him through?"

A few days later they do and Harold has the $5,000, which he quickly hands over to his daughter's boyfriend, a real-estate agent who, in turn, hands Harold the deed to a California orange grove.

Bissonette bundles his disgruntled wife, daughter, son, and dog into their jalopy and they leave New Jersey for the long drive West. Upon arriving in the neighborhood of his orange grove, Harold stops at a beautiful ranch and asks directions from its owner, Mr. Abernathy. Turns out Harold's place abuts Abernathy's grove. Harold's family now starts to get excited about their prospects, but are quickly confronted by reality when they see their new home. The groves stand fallow, the house is a dilapidated shack, and the only crop in sight consists of a dead twig rising from the ground. It bears what appears to be a single, shriveled raisin. Amelia has had it. She tells the children to follow her, and she starts to walk back to New Jersey, leaving Harold behind with the dog. Things are so bad Bissonette actually starts petting the mutt.

Suddenly Abernathy comes barreling up the dirt driveway in his truck. He jumps out and calls Harold a lucky man. Harold doesn't quite see it that way, but Abernathy tells him some tycoons want to build a racetrack and they need Bissonette's property for the grandstand. The promoters are on their way to negotiate for the property. Abernathy advises Harold to hold out for any price.

Sure enough, the money boys arrive in a fancy car. Amelia and the children return to investigate the ruckus. Harold withdraws a flask from the inside of his suit pocket and sucks in a mouthful.

The lead horse guy in the entourage of entrepreneurs opens negotiations at $5,000—the amount Harold paid for the dump in the first place.

Recalling his neighbor's advice, a confidant Bissonette takes a gulp from the flask and answers, "No!"

The racetrack promoter doubles the offer and tries flattery by praising Harold as a reasonable man and a hard bargainer.

Bissonette takes another pull on the flask. "No!"

Horse guy: "$15,000, and that's as high as I go!"

Harold hits the bottle again: "No!"

The promoter: "You're drunk!"

Bissonette:. "Yeah, and you're crazy. But, I'll be sober tomorrow, and you'll be crazy for the rest of your life."

Finally the promoter demands to know what Harold wants for the would-be cactus farm.

Bissonette sips from the flask, then corks it, puts it in his pocket, and pulls out the brochure that bears a photograph of the orange grove he thought he was buying.

Pointing to the picture, Harold says simply: "I want THIS orange ranch—and $40,000—no, $44,000! Mr. Abernathy needs his commission."

Crazy or not, the horse-track promoter meets Harold's price and both men leave happy with the deal. A classic win–win!

SUCCESSFUL NEGOTIATING

Master negotiators don't usually nip from the bottle while cutting a deal, but they do spend a lot of effort juggling the elements of time, power, and information—the three key factors in any negotiation.

Time

Understanding the role of time is essential. Often a negotiation will have an artificial timeframe. For example, a union contract may be set to expire at midnight on a certain date. When contract negotiations begin, both sides are likely to state the expiration date as the *absolute* date by which a new contract must be approved. Sometimes that's true, but often the deadline—like everything else—is taradiddle and becomes a point of negotiation. As the contract-expiration date draws near and negotiations stall, the opposing sides often agree to an extension. Their real deadline is usually marked not by a fixed date, but rather by the patience of the negotiators, the progress of the negotiations, and the goodwill of the parties. Both sides may have good reasons to extend the deadline. Management may want to keep its operations going because product demand is high. The union may want to keep its members on the job building its strike fund. Both sides may see advantages to offering, accepting, or conceding more at a later date than they would be willing to concede just to meet the "official" deadline.

Power

Clout, too, is critical—and is often the ultimate determinant of outcomes. In any negotiation, figure out if you or the other side has the clout. Again, let's look at a labor/management negotiation. If management has high inventories and is witnessing low prices and declining markets for its goods, it may be willing (indeed, anxious) to sustain long talks—even deal with a strike—because it has no compelling need to meet the union's demands. If, on the other hand, the company's inventories are low, its products are commanding high prices, and demand is exceeding production capacity, the company has an interest in avoiding slowdowns or work stoppages. It may want to settle quickly so it can maximize its returns in a boom market. In such a case, clout shifts to the union.

Looked at from the other side of the table, if the union's strike fund is low, loyalty to the union is weak, and the company's products are not in demand, the union lacks clout.

In any negotiation figure out if you or the other side has the clout. If the other person has a truncheon in hand, whilst your digits grab nothing and both of you know it . . . run! Whatever you do, do not fool yourself in your initial analysis. Too many people have walked to the negotiating table, confident of their clout only to find out, too late, that their clout was about out.

Information

Finally, the side that has the best information will cut the best deal. If all sides have equal information about themselves, their adversaries, and their market conditions, they can reason from a common set of facts and usually arrive at a mutually acceptable settlement. If one side knows more than the other does, however, the playing field is tilted in favor of the side with the most—and best—information.

Knowledge of the timing, clout, and facts around which a negotiation will evolve enables the parties to agree upon the style of negotiation that will occur. In most cases, one of three styles evolves: lose–lose, win–lose, and win–win. Obviously, in business the best deal for all concerned is a win–win. Too often, however, negotiators become entrenched and think only about win–lose, losing sight of the fact that fair-dealing at the bargaining table may ensure better future working relationships. Focus only on win–win!

Lose–lose outcomes involve compromise. Both sides give up more than they want to get less than they want. Labor/management negotiators often refer to this as the "price of industrial peace." Lose–lose outcomes usually mean that some external factor—such as high demand and high prices for a company's product—enable management to justify pay raises that everyone on the management team thinks are out of line in the long-term but necessary in the short-term; they also enable labor leaders to report that they "got most" of what they demanded. The larger issues are often postponed until a future contract negotiation. Not a good option.

Win–lose outcomes inevitably result when the sides are unevenly matched. Parent–child negotiations often fall into this category. In most cases, the parent holds all the cards: if Junior wants his allowance, he must keep his room clean. In business, if a company has excess inventory to carry it through the year and a union has an empty strike fund, the company holds all the cards—at least for a while. This enables the company to offer little or nothing at the table and the union has to bide its time and choke down the offered deal. In such cases, management breaks out the champagne and the employees swallow the bitter pill of defeat. (Oh, yes, in any win–lose situation the winner risks losing some important things: the respect, affection, and loyalty of the defeated. Those losses will often haunt the winner when the clout switches hands.) Still a lousy option!

Modern negotiating theory has focused increasingly on the possibilities inherent in win–win negotiating—which is particularly favored in sales-and-purchase situations. An example of this occurs when a company offers its services at Price A—a price it must command to maintain revenue growth and assure equity in its dealings within its customer base. A particularly difficult customer, however, may demand a special, lower price. In win–win negotiating the seller may propose options that meet the buyer's price point per unit in return for a higher volume of purchasing by the buyer. Or the seller may offer special advisory or promotional services as "value-added" incentives that entice the customer willing to abandon his price demands in return for greater value. In either case, both sides win: the vendor is able to maintain his pricing structure while the customer perceives that she's getting either the price she demanded or getting more value for the bucks she's spending.

Not every win–win strategy occurs during formal negotiations. In fact, many occur at the saloon . . . ah, supermarket . . . every time commodity prices drop for, say, pineapple juice. Instead of lowering the price of the bottle, the maker slightly increases its size. Ideally, the customer perceives that she's getting more juice for the jolt (value) for the same price, while the maker is able to maintain its gross income and price point. If the cost of pineapple juice has dropped by more than the cost of adding the extra amount to the bottle, the company actually *increases its margin* without alienating the customer. Everyone winds up happy!

In a true win–win situation, both sides go outside the parameters of the original situation and offer each other additional incentives that enable both bargainers to get *more* than they wanted!

Time, clout, and information represent leverage in any negotiation, and Harold Bissonette had them all on his side in *It's a Gift*.

First, Harold had a timing advantage. The track promoters were anxious to close the deal and get their track built. No doubt, their investors were antsy. Harold, on the other hand, had all the time in the world—and nothing to lose since he'd just lost everything. He also had a nice timing prop, maintaining his calm with that flask of "calming cider."

Second, although the promoters had the money, Harold had the land. At worst, the clout factor was equal. Harold knew that his chunk of desert was needed just to hold the grand-stands. Evidently, the racetrack folk had previously acquired all other needed parcels. Harold had real clout: Without his land the syndicate's previous expenditures would be worthless. Talk about leverage!

Finally, Harold had excellent information. Abernathy had given Bissonette the inside scoop, so he not only knew the racing syndicate's plan, but also that they needed him to complete their acquisition. Harold also knew that the pro-moters had the money to meet his price.

COUNTING YOUR CARDS

There is a certain card player's mentality when it comes to negotiating. You have to know when to hold, when to fold, and when to bluff.

Consider this example, from Fields's career. In 1938, Paramount Studios cut Fields loose due to his inability to work homogeneously with his directors, producers, and any-one who thought he or she knew the art better than W. C. did. So W. C. offered his services to the highest-bidding studio. In that decade Fields's films raked in the greatest profit. Paramount was on a roll in the thirties and could afford to jettison any troublemaker, even financially successful ones. On the other hand, Universal Studios was in serious financial trouble. Universal needed to borrow money, and to get a loan they needed a proven star who could carry a movie on his or her name alone. The story goes that the Bank of America agreed to advance Universal the cash it needed with one stipulation: Universal had to sign Fields. W. C. caught wind of the negotiations, and he didn't fold; he held out for an astronomical salary, to which the bank and the studio agreed. In 1938, W. C. Fields became the sixth highest-salaried individual in the United States.

In the Universal case, life imitated art. Fields's negotiating style in the Universal deal resembles closely that of Harold's in *It's a Gift*. Fields benefited from time (Universal had to act fast; Fields didn't); clout (Universal was desperate; Fields had box-office power—exactly what the studio needed); and Fields had great information (he knew that he had to be part of Universal's deal with the bank).

By applying the lessons from *It's a Gift* to his real-life negotiations with Universal, Fields did what every good negotiator should do: He reviewed a previous negotiation to gain knowledge for a future negotiation. That made things better not only for W. C. and Universal but also for the audiences who saw Fields in the great films that followed.

Of course, three years later when Fields's contract expired, the now fabulously successful studio no longer needed its fabulously successful but contentious star. Fate, timing, and luck have a lot to do with successful negotiating . . . and card playing. Even clout will turn.

W. C.'S TOP FIVE TIPS FOR NEGOTIATING ANYTHING

1. Always know what you want, and the "Proof."
2. Timing is everything! Unless you're asleep.
3. Never let THEM know what YOU know they know.
4. When in doubt, pause (with or without a swig of "pineapple juice") and just say, "No!"
5. Sometimes you have to take a chance even while negotiating. Don't be afraid. Remember, "Lady Godiva put everything she had on a horse."

Certainly office politics often demands kissing . . . your boss's . . . ah . . . hand. Here W. C. and Leon Errol kiss the hand of Susan Miller in this posed shot from Never Give a Sucker an Even Break.

CHAPTER NINE

OFFICE POLITICS

"IF AT FIRST YOU DON'T SUCCEED, TRY, TRY AGAIN . . . THEN GIVE UP! NO SENSE IN MAKING A FOOL OF YOURSELF!"

IN HIS FINEST SCREEN ROLE, FIELDS (AS MR. Micawber in *David Copperfield*) works for one of the great white-collar villains of all time, the oily, deceitful, and falsely "'umble" Uriah Heep. Heep is ever accommodating, adept at flattery, and never tires of performing obsequious little tasks for his aging boss, whom he backstabs, blindsides, bamboozles, and manipulates until the poor boss is on the verge of losing his business—to Heep.

Fortunately, Micawber, who reports to Heep and has been a patient, passive, but disapproving observer of Uriah's shenanigans, decides enough is enough. He finds evidence that sends Uriah Heep to the dust heap. In Micawber's case, this shows that an honest man can cheat a cheat—giving hope to all future whistleblowers and weasel silencers.

All who meet Heep know he's a weasel, but they fail to confront his perfidy until his excesses really threaten the business. If they'd held a vote, not a single person associated with the business would have voted for Heep as the boss's successor. Heep didn't feel he needed their support. He thought he needed only the boss's support, but in the end, if you float flattery falsely too often it will buy you nothing but disdain. Politeness, brains, and sincerity will always win over dirty politics. Believe in your points, argue them honestly, and accept the compromise cheerfully. That's successful office politics in a nutshell.

If you think politics shouldn't matter, you're defining "dirty" politics only. We hate the popular bromide, "They're just playing politics." Every time we interact with another human being, we play politics, and God save us if we did not. Politics is the art of compromise; the art of persuasion; the ability to politely negotiate a settlement between two divergent points of view. Nations play it, neighbors play it, husbands and wives and sisters and brothers play it. It keeps the murder rate low.

Dirty politics, on the other hand, attempts to achieve the same end through lying, cheating, and stealing as observed and commented upon by our hero, W. C. Fields. (Sitting in a cafeteria Fields defends a comment he made about the meal he just ate, "I didn't squawk about the steak, dear. I merely said I didn't see that old horse that used to be tethered outside here." That's dirty politics. It's a lie! But you have to love it! It avoided a potentially nasty confrontation.)

In the office we play personal politics, but we also play corporate politics. Corporate or organizational politics is merely the collection of techniques—some constructive, some destructive—groups use to arrive at important decisions after weighing a variety of choices. The way politics is played in any organization is determined by the style of the corporation's top leaders, the traditions of the company, and the presence or absence of rules governing the decision-making process.

Some organizations are more democratic than others; some are more open and inclusive than others; some are more structured and process-oriented than others. The first rule of corporate politics: Know the rules that govern decision making. And the second rule: Know who holds the ultimate decision-making power. In some cases a committee holds the power; in others one person controls all decisions, an autocracy where the head muck-a-muck makes the final decision and can overrule any preliminary decisions. Few organizations are truly democratic, or autocratic; most are democratic at some level and autocratic at other levels of decision making. But in *You Can't Cheat an Honest Man*, the Whipsnade circus entertains no democracy at any level. That grand despot Larsen E. Whipsnade, the larcenous leader of the traveling show, makes all of the decisions without consultation. You play politics by doing everything he tells you without question, or you get fired.

When we think of politics in a pejorative sense we associate the word with insincere flattery, unfairness, chicanery, misuse of power—and poor results. The Great McGonigle in *The Old Fashioned Way* leads with just such cozenage. He heads a mutinous band of traveling thespians. As their train pulls into Belfontaine, their next engagement, Fields pretends to read a telegram that alleges their upcoming show has been sold out in advance. This slight deceit creates nothing but derision and Bronx cheers from his little troupe, who obviously heard the same old unfulfilled promises many times before. Mark Anthony McGonigle ignores their dis-pleasure and pushes on, "I won't be surprised if there was a brass band awaiting our arrival." More hoots! By coincidence and to McGonigle's utter surprise, a brass band plays as the train comes to a stop. Unfortunately, it plays for some dignitary who also happens to be on the train, but that does not stop McGonigle from parading his troupe through the streets of Belfontaine where absolutely no one takes notice.

The point: If you want to have influence within your organization, you must engage in politics, but that doesn't mean you have to be a weasel or a phony. It does mean you have to realize that no one died and made you God and that if you want to get something done, you are going to have to have the support of other people, work with them sincerely, and compromise for the good of the whole.

Learning to consistently play the right kind of office politics will also help get you promoted. In most organizations there is no formal "election" process governing who gets a promotion and rises through the ranks of an organization, but there is always an informal election. This means you must, if you want to be an effective wielder of influence, prove yourself not only to your boss, but also to your peers and colleagues.

POLITICS IN ACTION

Let's look at a successful outcome to a political battle over succession to the chief operating officer's job. This example is based on a true story, but the company asked us to keep its name out of it. Here's how the battle was resolved.

When the COO took early retirement for health reasons, six competent, ambitious, and fiercely competitive subordinates vied for the job. After considering each of their strengths and weaknesses, the CEO, knowing he needed all of their talents and tired of hearing them cut each other down when he interviewed them, decided to take a democratic approach to the problem—he'd hold an election. (He did, however, tell the candidates the vote was advisory, not binding, and reserved the right to overrule the results.)

The CEO prepared ballots and asked each person to cast a vote to pick the next COO. What a coincidence! Each of the six received one vote! ("It baffles science!") So a second election was held. This time the six were asked to vote for *two* people. To be valid, a ballot had to contain the names of two of the candidates.

The results looked like this (names changed to protect the guilty):

J. Augustus Winterbottom: One vote for himself and one vote for J. Frothingell Bellows

J. Frothingell Bellows: One vote for himself and one vote for Flower Belle Lee

Flower Belle Lee: One vote for herself and one vote for Bellows

Oulietta Delight Hemoglobin: One vote for herself and one vote for Winterbottom

Cuthbert J. Twillie: (Recognizing that he would probably get no votes other than his own, which would be neutralized, submitted a blank ballot because he didn't believe any of the other candidates were qualified): No vote (And good luck at your next job!)

Loudmouth McNasty: One vote for himself and one vote for Bellows

The CEO gave the six a short time to campaign, and they spent that time lobbying one another. The campaigns themselves give us some insight into corporate politics.

Winterbottom, for example, offered incentives, telling the others "If I get the job, I'll take care of you." That was enough to get the second vote of just one of the other candidates. The others were insulted by what they considered a blatant attempt at bribery and decided against Winterbottom.

Bellows was the clear favorite. In effect the candidates were saying, "if it can't be me, I think Bellows would be the best choice."

The CEO announced the top three candidates, but didn't announce how they had fared. Then he took a third and final vote among the three contenders only. Winterbottom, Bellows, and Lee were allowed to cast two votes (ballots bearing the same name twice would be disqualified). The final tally: Bellows got 3 votes, Lee got 2 votes, and Winterbottom got one 1 vote (his own).

Bellows, of course, got the job—even though the CEO had initially favored McNasty. The CEO reasoned that if McNasty did not have the confidence of his peers, he would make a poor leader.

We know of another company that used this election method to promote an employee, but the voters included key subordinates of the candidates. It was interesting to see how many people apparently did not vote for the advancement of their immediate supervisors, but then again, we doubt that any of the actors in The Great McGonigle's troupe would vote favorably for their immediate supervisor. ("Drat their hides!")

(Fields once said that he had never voted *for* anyone. "I always vote against!")

In our example the CEO's process worked because each candidate realized that he or she could wind up working for the eventual winner and thus had to decide whom he or she would find most acceptable.

Bellows told the others that he would work to be fair, discussed some of the questions he had about his own performance, explained that he had enjoyed working with them, and finally that he would need their talents and support in developing a new vision for the company if he got the job. (This was neither taradiddle nor folderol. Bellows's sincerity showed through.)

Flower Belle Lee argued that she had earned the job because she'd been with the company the longest.

Ms. Hemoglobin argued that she was the oldest candidate and therefore, if elected, would be retiring soon, opening up opportunities for the others to succeed to the top at a relatively early date.

Twillie alienated most of the others when he argued that he had the boss's support and that they should vote for him because he'd likely get the job anyway since the vote was "only advisory."

McNasty, the financial officer, argued that the company was not paying enough attention to cost controls and that if any of them were going to have jobs in the future, his leadership would put the company on a sound footing by making sure costs were contained. When asked about other aspects of his vision for the company, he said he'd deal with vision once the costs were controlled.

The final count was 0 votes for Twillie, 2 votes for Winterbottom, 4 votes for Bellows, 2 votes for Flower Belle Lee, and 1 vote each for candidates Hemoglobin and McNasty (now there's a name for a law firm!).

In the end the process adopted by the CEO not only got him the right person for the job, but also gave each of the candidates a chance to build a relationship with the successful candidate. He had recognized that the ability of his successor to lead the company would derive, in part, from the consent and support of the other leaders in the company; a simple autocratic appointment would have left resentment and rancor. Very smart! A great example of good politics. Of course, if this process appeared in a Fields film the ballot box would have been stuffed.

Personal and organizational politics works only when a high level of goodwill and respect exists among the partisans of competing viewpoints. When individuals and groups argue about a specific approach their company takes to a problem, they must not disagree about one thing: rules of disagreement and the decision-making process. If you disagree on how you express your disagreement, you will unleash the destructive aspects of politics: petty rifts arise and backstabbing thrives, resulting in decaying morale and productivity.

In office politics every leader and would-be leader would be well served to remember this piece of advice from W. C.'s book *Fields for President.* Speaking from the point of view of a voter, he said: "Remember we are more numerous than you are."

W. C.'S POLITICAL HANDBOOK

When it comes to a vote, you want to be everybody's second choice (after themselves). If at first you don't succeed, try, try again . . . then give up. No sense making a damn fool of yourself.

- Remember THEY are more numerous than you are.
- Start every day with a smile and get it over with!
- I never vote *for* anyone. I always vote against.
- Upon meeting the mayor of his hometown: "It's an honor, your honor. I voted for you in the last election . . . several times."
- "Silence, weasel!"
- Nip little weasels and little snakes in the bud before they become big snakes, "They were only young snakes . . . even if they bite you, you wouldn't die."

"Count your change before leaving the window." In this rehearsal shot from
You Can't Cheat an Honest Man, *Fields's leg breaks through the trap door in his ticket booth.
Added in the final shoot was a dog, a W. C. life-long nemesis, which sneaks underneath
the circus wagon and chews W. C.'s foot as he transacts business.*

CHAPTER TEN

EFFECTIVE COMMUNICATION

W. C. FIELDS NEVER ATTENDED HIGH SCHOOL, YET he became a master stylist in both written and spoken English. W. C. took great delight in uncommon and archaic words, using them to prick the balloon of pomposity (or, as he might well have said, "the dirigibles of ostentation," "the Zeppelins of the magniloquent," or "airs of the arrogant employers of argot"). He also used them whenever he was playing a shady character. Invariably, when W. C. launches into a tall tale, he inflates his language, adopting the rolling polysyllables of the snake-oil salesman, bunko artist, and carnival barker. As a street-smart hustler, W. C. learned early on that obscure and flowery language is the bait with which every con man sets his hook when he's fishing for suckers.

He always carried and studied the dictionary. He enjoyed looking for euphemisms with which to enrich his routines. The euphemisms, along with W. C.'s penchant for cobbling together strange-sounding names, were a hallmark of his comedy. Here are some examples of "Fieldspeak":

- A taxi takes off . . . "like a bat from the habitat of Old Ned."
- He refers to his nose as . . . "my scarlet proboscis."
- He calls Charlie McCarthy "a termite's picnic," "son of a gate-leg table," "the woodpecker's poster boy," "stunted spruce," "diminutive bundling board."
- He refers to beloved female companions as "my little chickadee," "my phlox, my flower."

In a previous chapter, we explored Fields's use of language in terms of creativity. Here we mention it, not because it was inventive, but because it added impact and personality to his communications. In Fields's hands, a euphemism was an education in itself; it defined and clarified, rather than muddied meaning. Fields was a prolific correspondent, and he wrote classic complaint letters, thank-you letters, and letters soliciting roles. E-mail may make it easier to send an effective message, but it doesn't make it easier to write one. This is one area in which Fields offers countless examples on how to do it "write" and say it with style and clarity.

COMMUNICATING COURTEOUSLY

We link communications and courtesy in the same chapter because knowing *when* to communicate is every bit as important as *how* to communicate—particularly when thank-you's, apologies, condolences, and acknowledgments are required.

We consulted with our fictional, but nonetheless qualified, etiquette expert, Mrs. Hermosillo Brunch (we named her after a character in one of Fields's films). Our topic: communication protocols. "Any nincompoop can master the basics," Mrs. Brunch said. According to her there are five rules:

1. *Reply promptly.* With rare exceptions, Mrs. Brunch (as did W. C.) responds to letters within 48 hours of their receipt. Phone calls are returned within 24 hours. E-mails requiring response are acknowledged within eight hours. Cigars received are lighted immediately.

2. *Be specific.* "Obscurity wastes time and fosters confusion," says Mrs. Brunch. "Please speak and write to the point." Fields's letters invariably stuck to his topic. The rambling digressions that mark his comic speeches and essays contrast sharply with the focus and concise use of language in his letters.

3. *Have style.* "Always write as if you were speaking to an intelligent friend," says Mrs. Brunch. "Do this even if your own friends are not very intelligent. Mr. Fields's letters always sounded like Mr. Fields. They were never soulless, nor did they suffer from 'computer generation,' which I consider one of the technological diseases. His tone varied by topic—he could be quite nasty, you know—but it always matched perfectly his purpose."

4. *Don't just respond; initiate communication.* "This is particularly important when someone has done something you like," Mrs. Brunch told us. Mr. Fields

routinely sent a kind note when a colleague related a particularly funny story or acknowledged him with a gift, card, or the thing he valued most: a favorable public comment or review.

5. *Respond in the appropriate medium.* Mrs. Brunch believes in responding in kind. "If you receive a personal letter by mail, you should reply by mail," she says. "Even when, for time's sake, you must fax a response, you should always mail an original. Likewise, e-mail should be answered by e-mail, phone calls by phone calls. There are many exceptions, of course." Mrs. Brunch is adamant on one point. "Remember always that some things are best done the old-fashioned way. This applies, in particular, to short thank-you notes. It took me years to teach this simple lesson to my husband, who insisted upon sending dictated, typewritten thank-you notes—even to friends—on his company letterhead. Heavens! They looked like form letters! Mr. Brunch sometimes now receives 'thank-you's' for his thank-you's. People are so pleasantly surprised these days to receive handwritten notes. Even if your penmanship is as sloppy as my husband's, the note will mean more because the recipient will know you took the time to write it yourself!"

COMMUNICATING INTELLIGENTLY

Good communications is more than a matter of letters, of course, but if you practice writing "intelligent letters to friends," you'll soon find yourself speaking more intelligently to them as well.

Here are a few examples of W. C.'s letters (real ones) that illustrate the principles Mrs. Brunch discussed.

A Letter of Protest and Assurance

To Adolph Zukor, April 22, 1938

To give you an illustration of what I get up against with comic writers: A writer on one of my recent pictures suggested a routine, in fact, he had the whole routine written out and when he was informed that it was my routine and I had used it in the last picture, he laughed heartily and said: "Christ, I forgot where I stole that one from." This is only one of many instances where writers have taken whole scenes from my former pictures and tried to sell them to me again. Most of these writers do not go to the trouble of even varying the dialogue or the situation in the slightest.

Please be assured, Mr. Zukor, that I will work conscientiously and with as much speed as it is possible and give you material that will not cause the company any added expense in fighting plagiarism suits.

A Letter of Thanks

To Jack Benny, April 16, 1941

Dear Friend Jack:

Many thanks for giving your permission to use the Albuquerque episode from your broadcast some while ago.

I never miss your air show and it seems that I appreciate it all the more with every broadcast. I feel that I am in with you and Mary and Rochester, Dennis and his mother, Phil, Don, Andy, Schlep, and it's something to look forward to on Sunday evening. Best wishes and thanks from your fan.

A Humorous Response

Our last example needs a bit of explanation. On June 19, 1941, Valerie Caravacci, from Charles Beyer's Agency, which represented W.C., sent Fields a news photo of Hitler, Mussolini and an unidentified Nazi, all giving the fascist salute. She identified them—joking, of course—as clients the agency had just signed and inquired if W.C., a notorious Nazi-hater, could help them find work in motion pictures. Two days later, Fields responded:

Dear Miss Caravacci: (Miss Valerie)

Your letter with the enclosed wire photo of Mussolini, Hitler and a friend of Hitler's all asking to go to the bathroom was more than a surprise to me.

If you have any more obscene literature or photographs, will you please bring them up personally so that neither of us gets into difficulties with the postal authorities?

My very best wishes, and please do be careful, dear.

Sincerely,

W. C. Fields

Now that's a great letter: funny, defensive, and concerned—and shorter than the Gettysburg Address!

W. C. GETS IT WRITE

1. No cliché exists that cannot be improved upon. If *you* can't improve it, don't use it!

2. When I use a word, it means what I choose it to mean, neither more nor less.

3. The question is whether you can make words mean different things. The answer is "yes"! It's called Spin.

4. The question is which is to be the master, you or the word, that's all!

5. Find a younger, single, better-looking etiquette expert to provide same advice regarding protocols. Perhaps Miss Oulietta Delight Hemoglobin is available!

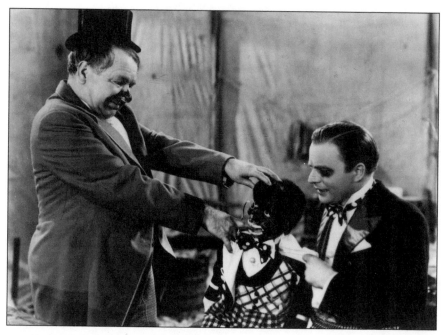

"Return my primary digit, you woodpecker's lunch." That's Charlie McCarthy and Edgar Bergen. It was Charlie who once said, "Isn't it true, Mr. Fields, that 43 cars stop on Hollywood and Vine waiting for your nose to turn green?" This photo comes from the Universal film You Can't Cheat an Honest Man.

CHAPTER ELEVEN

DEALING WITH DIFFICULT PEOPLE

Don't be a Fuddy-Duddy! Don't be a Mooncalf! Don't be a Jabbernowl! You're not one of those are you?

DIFFICULT PEOPLE HAVE ONE TRAIT IN COMMON: They drive everyone crazy and create continual tension in the workplace. They thrive on conflict, particularly when they can light the fuses of others and then sit back while they explode. As bosses, they are like Fields's character in *The Dentist:* They tell you to do something, and as soon as you've done it, they say you should have done something else. Some are shrewish naggers; some are unmotivated themselves and therefore try to demotivate everyone around them. Some are merely procrastinators or malingerers. Some are hypochondriacs. Some are mythomaniacs—"people who believe that anything they say is true so therefore they can say anything and it will be true." They can't distinguish truth from their self-created myths.

When we see such types in a Fields film, they are funny. In the workplace, they are not. W. C.'s movies are filled with these crazy makers—and Fields plays many of them himself. The list of "difficult people" is almost as long as Fields's formidable filmography. As *The Dentist*, he plays a mean, nasty, petty tyrant. In *The Bank Dick*, he plays a credit-mongering, mythomaniacal layabout who uses his position to arrange the theft and cover-up of funds. In *You're Telling Me*, W. C.'s a hapless and bibulous inventor. In *The Big Broadcast of 1938* he plays the accident-prone, bumbling brother of a tycoon (bad luck follows him like smoke follows a cigar). As the President of Klopstokia, Fields is an irascible, paranoid tyrant. As Ambrose Wolfinger in *The Man on the Flying Trapeze*, W. C. takes part of the day off (with pay) to moonlight on company time. As Micawber in *David Copperfield*, he relies on his faith that "something will turn up" to carry him through life, never seeking to control his own destiny until the very end of the film where he finally takes control and reveals Heep as a criminal.

Fields isn't the only difficult person in his movies. The casts are also filled with supporting characters whose attitudes can slowly wear away at the productivity of any office: shrews, "princes" and "princesses," dunderheads, and liars. There are also brats (epitomized by Baby LeRoy), smart-alecks (particularly Charlie McCarthy), mooncalves and blockheads (often played to slow-witted perfection by young Grady Sutton), fuddy-duddies (one of them is named Mrs. Dunk), and office sirens (like *Million-Dollars Legs*'s Mata Machree, "the woman no man can resist").

Off screen, Fields could be more difficult than the characters in his movies. Perversely abrupt mood changes, hypersensitivity to slights, and a jealous attitude to the success of others who might "steal" a scene from him drove people he worked with, as well as those he worked for, crazy. We've previously told you about W. C.'s battle with Mae West during the filming of *My Little Chickadee*. That was an aggressive but reasonable competition, given that Miss West was a strong woman who was known for giving as good as she got in such exchanges. W. C.'s relationship with "that Trojan infant," Baby LeRoy is another matter. Fields and Baby LeRoy, (Ronald Leroy Overacker) made three films together: *The Old-Fashioned Way, Tillie and Gus,* and *It's a Gift.*

BATTLING THE BABY

In *The Old-Fashioned Way,* Paramount whipped up a publicity-driven fabrication of a feud between Fields and Baby LeRoy. Paramount claimed they reserved 40 square feet of space on a wall so Fields could post his complaints about the child. Presumably, it was all in fun. But on the set, sometimes one couldn't be sure. There's a scene in which Fields is supposed to give the kid a kick in the fundament. In the first cut, W. C. kicked so hard he sent LeRoy sailing across the stage. Reports vary from 6 to 15 feet! Eyewitnesses confirm that this was no love tap, but it seemed Leroy and W. C. both knew it was for fun. Nevertheless, Paramount, fearing audience protest, wanted the scene lopped from the film, but Fields fought to keep it in. They compromised and Fields promised that if the scene were reshot he would not kick LeRoy so hard. Paramount agreed—and this time LeRoy was just slightly lifted off the ground. When asked why he fought so hard to keep the scene in the film, W. C. responded, "There's not a man in the world who hasn't had a secret desire to boot a kid!"

Despite the tensions over the kicking incident, Fields insisted on working with the kid in his next movie. During auditions for *It's a Gift*, Fields asked that Baby LeRoy be cast as the child. The studio was reluctant. They thought LeRoy was too old (at age two-and-a-half!). Having worked on two previous movies, Fields knew the youngster's abilities to steal scenes. Maybe W. C. was feeling guilty about the kicks he'd delivered the kid in *The Old-Fashioned Way*; or perhaps he believed the scene-stealing devil he knew was better than a new box-office baby. Or, perhaps, he wanted to kick the kid again! In any event, Fields's intervention got LeRoy the job. What a nice Mr. Fields! Once shooting started, it was different: Fields found LeRoy irritating not only because he was a scene-stealing threat (the brat!) but also because he could break out into screeching tears (no doubt like fingernails scraping a blackboard for the easily irritated Fields).

Then there is the story of W. C. having once spiked LeRoy's orange juice or milk. After years of researching the matter, I can tell you the versions you've heard have been substantially embellished. Here, to the best of my knowledge, is what really happened: The "Trojan infant," as W. C. called him, was in a cantankerous mood during the filming of *It's a Gift*. The kid was crying, wailing, and holding up production. His nurse fed LeRoy his bottle in an effort to calm him down. Fields then came over to help, asking the nurse if he could feed the little nipper. The nurse obliged. After a few minutes, W. C. asked the nurse if she would slip across the street to a newsstand and pick up a copy of the *Daily Racing Form*. She agreed. While she was gone, Fields dropped a little gin in the bottle before he resumed feeding the baby. LeRoy sucked it up and then passed out. The kid was out for the day and shooting was cancelled. As Fields walked off the set, he yelled to the director, "I told you the kid was no trouper!" (Actually, LeRoy eventually proved to be quite a trooper. When his child-acting days were over, he continued his theatrical training, later playing adult roles in about a dozen films.)

HARD TO HANDLE

W. C. was difficult even when others weren't stealing his scenes. Fields consistently pushed hard to get his signature pool shooting and golf acts worked into his movies. Sometimes he succeeded, sometimes not, but he was both insistent and persistent in his requests. Aware of Fields's desire—and before Fields could ask him—director Eddie Sutherland offered W. C. a chance to work the pool act into the 1935 film version of *Poppy.* Sutherland approached Fields with the presumed good news. The director explained that he had to make a lot of changes in the script in order to insert the scene, which would give W. C. a special showcase for his talents. But Fields astounded Sutherland by saying he wouldn't do the scene. Asked why, Fields said, "It wouldn't fit the plot . . . directors are always trying to get me to do something like that—and it throws everything off balance." (This, of course, had never previously stopped Fields from requesting the insertion of such scenes.) Sutherland reported that he had already told the producer, Arthur Hornblow, Jr., that Fields would do the scene.

"Well, untell him," Fields said. "Producers are all bums anyway."

Sutherland tried to "untell" Hornblow, but the producer decided to talk to W. C. himself. Fields listened as Hornblow begged him to insert the scene, noting that he, as producer, and Sutherland, as director, had knocked themselves out trying to find a place for the pool scene. Having appealed to W. C.'s sense of guilt, Hornblow then appealed to his ego. The producer argued that W. C. owed his public a chance to again see the great routine and that it would be especially appreciated by younger audiences who had never seen it. Fields acted surprised by Hornblow's pleadings. Of course he would do the scene, Fields said, "I'd be a fool not to do it." He and Hornblow shook hands and Hornblow departed. A few minutes later, Sutherland approached Fields and found him whistling. Sutherland said "Bill, you haven't any intention of doing that scene, do you?" Fields stopped whistling just long enough to say "not in the least." Then Sutherland asked "What prompted you to mislead the producer?" W. C. replied, 'Ah, the hell with the old buzzard,' he said, and left to get a drink." Fields was difficult.

PREVENTING PEOPLE PROBLEMS

W. C. Fields's movies and life present quite a collection: drunks, wisecrackers, naysayers, taradiddlers, Trojan infants, weasels, sirens, grumpy old men, naggers, layabouts, procrastinators, and obfuscators.

That same list of difficult people show up in all businesses. One would wonder who hired these people, except that most of us have hired more than a few ourselves. Some difficult employees are difficult from day one on the job. Sometimes this is simply a matter of poor hiring. Sometimes it's because the new person lacks experience in adjusting to the demands of the workplace, a particular problem of young employees in the early portion of their careers. But most "problem employees" were once excellent employees who have hit the skids. Sometimes the slide is precipitous, brought on by an extramarital affair, drunkenness, or financial problems. In most cases, however, the slide is slow and its increments are difficult to perceive until they culminate over months or years into consistently below-par performance that suddenly becomes obvious.

If you want to minimize the difficulties you face from difficult employees, there are five stages at which you can do damage control and prevention.

1. *Hiring.* Do proper screening and take time to find the right person; it will save you lots of trouble later. When the bank "rewards" Egbert Sousé thinking he has foiled a robbery, they seem not to care that Sousé has a rather lousy reputation. Apparently they do no background check. The only thing they seem to know about him is that he doesn't pay his bills (they know that because of his tardy mortgage payments).

2. *Defining Expectations.* Make sure the person knows the expectations of the job and that you have described them well from day one on the job. People become demoralized when they don't know what their job entails or what standards they are expected to uphold.

3. *Monitoring performance regularly.* You can't maintain performance standards without a process for measuring how people are doing—and letting them know where they stand. Regular and precise performance evaluations are necessary for this. The evaluation must be shared with the employee if it's to do any good, and the employee must feel that the process is designed to be constructive.

4. *Retraining and remotivating.* If someone "goes bad" midcareer and you value the person's past contributions and believe he or she has future ones to make, you can retrain and attempt to reinspire your employee to new heights—or at least adequate ones. Encourage and require training that is designed to broaden employee perspectives on business life cycles, creativity in the workplace, and the importance of working with and through others.

5. *Firing.* The ultimate action in dealing with "difficult people" is dismissal. Firing people is fraught with potential trouble. Do it wrongly and you'll be sued. If you must fire someone, it's as much a reflection on management's failure as on the employee's. Firing on the basis of poor performance or attitude sometimes means that hiring practices need to be improved, that job descriptions and performance evaluation processes are failing, that training is lacking, or that motivational skills are inadequate.

101

CHAPTER
ELEVEN
*Dealing with
Difficult
People*

W. C.'S GUIDE TO DIFFICULT PEOPLE

Type	Description	Example	How to Deal With
Jabbernowl	A stupid person; blockhead	Grady Sutton as Chester in *You Can't Cheat an Honest Man*	Put in charge when you're away from circus; stupidity can be an asset
Fuddy-duddy	An old-fashioned, pompous person, overly concerned with trifles; unimaginative	The Bel-Goodie Clan in *You Can't Cheat an Honest Man*	Tell them you're with the circus and they'll go away
Mooncalf	A simpleton; a foolish or absent-minded person	Grady Sutton, as Cuthbert in *The Pharmacist*	Be kind. He's probably your future son-in-law
Curmudgeon	A crusty, ill-tempered, and usually old man	Fields as *The Dentist* (among many others)	Don't be his caddy; do be his bartender!
Siren	Temptress; an insidiously seductive woman	Lyda Roberti as Mata Machree in *Million Dollar Legs*	Assign to Sweetheart, the only manager who can resist "the woman no man can resist."
Trojan infant	Scene-stealing up-and-comer	Baby LeRoy in anything	A noggin of gin in his bottle
Smart alecks	An obnoxiously self-assertive person	Charlie McCarthy in anything	Sandpaper works wonders; be skilled with hand-saw

Usually crisis management means teaming up with someone to overcome an impending problem. In If I Had a Million, *Fields and Skipworth team up to battle road hogs. Nearly all business crises require a team approach to solve.*

CHAPTER TWELVE

CRISIS MANAGEMENT

WHEN A CRISIS HITS, EVERYONE ASSOCIATED WITH IT becomes a crisis manager. Routines are cast to the winds, creating ripples of crisis throughout an organization as the "big problem" absorbs all the attention. Of course, we have degrees of crises. There's the huge kind, the kind that can cost you a major customer, damage your company's reputation, or wreck your business:

- A cook underbroils the hamburgers, causing an outbreak of e-coli.

- A disgruntled employee or psychopathic consumer poisons some over-the-counter medicine.

104

NEVER GIVE A
SUCKER AN EVEN
BREAK
*W. C. Fields on
Business*

- A tanker runs aground and the resulting oil spill damages fishing grounds, destroys wildlife habitat, and sends tourism into a downspin.

- A minor malfunction at a nuclear plant causes a series of events that leads to a near meltdown.

- You run a corner store like Fields did in *It's a Gift* and in comes Mr. Muckle, the blind and deaf hotel detective and a man very dangerous around glassware. Meanwhile you can't muster the courage to tell another customer who wants kumquats that you don't carry kumquats.

Not all crises are that big!

Take *The Bank Dick* as an example. Fields plays Egbert Sousé (no, that's not souse, it's Sousé, accent over the final "e"), who works diligently as an unemployed, dipsomaniacal bumbler. He easily garners disrespect from his two daughters and well-deserved harassment from his wife and mother-in-law.

Then his fate changes. Falsely credited with having caught the Lompoc bank robbers, Egbert, the ersatz hero, stumbles into employment, landing the job of bank detective, or Bank Dick, at the very same Lompoc Bank. While on the job for just a couple of days, a con man convinces Sousé that a fortune awaits him if he would only buy some Beefstake mine stocks. Sousé finds himself cash poor, but persuades his soon-to-be son-in-law, Og Oggilby, a bank clerk, to "borrow" $500 from the bank's vault. The son-in-law balks. He doesn't want to take the chance, but Sousé uses irrefutable logic on the boy: "Take a chance! Take it while you're young. My uncle, a balloon ascensionist, Effingham Huffnagel, took a chance. He was three and a half miles up in the air. He jumped out of the basket of the balloon and took a chance of alighting on a load of hay." Og: "Did he make it?" Egbert: "Ah . . . no . . . no, he didn't. Had he been a younger man he probably would have made it. That's the point—don't wait too long in life." Sold to the man whose name "Sounds like a bubble in a bathtub." Og plans to replace the money at week's end, when his salary check arrives. The next day, a crisis arrives instead. It comes in the form of the fastidious J. Pinkerton Snoopington (played by the inimitable Franklin Pangborn), bank examiner.

Facing this crisis, Sousé takes quick action. First, he drags Snoopington off to "The Black Pussy Cat Café." (Actually the censors made him name it that, but Fields refers to it consistently as "The Black Pussy Café"). In any event, he asks the bartender if Michael Finn as been in lately (a mickey by any other name). The bartender assures him, "No, but he will be soon." Fields orders the drinks, and the bartender drops a few granules of the knockout drug into Snoopington's glass. A couple of sips later, Snoopington becomes deathly ill. Egbert carries him back to his hotel room, puts him to bed, and calls on the services of Dr. Stall, a quack of the first degree. Stall prescribes a diet of castor oil and, on Sousé's urgings, four days of bed rest, just enough time for Og to return the funds. Crisis managed, you say? Not so fast; Snoopington is dedicated. Despite doctor's orders he shows up at the bank the next day.

"Mr. Sousé," the examiner explains, "if duty called I would go into the tsetse fly country of Africa and brave sleeping sickness if there were books to be examined." Crisis management mode once again! Sousé tries a few more dilatory measures. First, he smashes Snoopy's right hand in an old check press. "That'll interfere with your writing, won't it?" Nope!

Snoopington is left-handed! When Snoopington drops his glasses on the floor, Sousé steps on them. "I hope that won't interfere with your auditing the books." It won't. Snoopington carries an entire case of extra spectacles! By now, the examiner's suspicions are aroused and discovery of the pilferage seems a foregone conclusion. Sousé's "crisis-management" techniques have failed! But then dumb luck takes over . . . The con man sweeps into the bank and wants to buy the stocks back from Og. Crisis over? Not exactly! Just before the transfer can be finalized, Sousé reads the *Lompoc Picayune-Inteligenser* that announces in banner headlines, "The Beefstake Mines a Bonanza!" Fields socks the con man on the proboscis and knocks him out. The mine has struck pay dirt, and the bonds are worth enough to cover the "loan" and make Sousé and his son-in-law fabulously wealthy! Then luck turns sour again. A new crisis! The bank is robbed for the second time! After a great chase scene, in which Sousé finds himself driving the getaway car at gunpoint, Sousé reaches the end of the road at the shores of a vast lake. But, unbeknownst to him, the robber has long since been rendered unconscious after hitting a low-slung tree branch as he stood in the back seat of the convertible. Turns out the bandit, Repulsive Rogan, had a bounty on the robber's head. Sousé earns another reward. Crisis over! With the reward, and the proceeds of the mining stock, Egbert Sousé retires to a lovely estate and the now-loving affections of wife and family. All because he had the good sense to manage crisis after crisis . . . and a bit of Hollywood-only luck!

Crisis and conflict are the twin pillars around which good stories—and good movies—revolve. But they can spell death for a business. Fields's films—and his career—are filled with crises, big and small.

- In *You Can't Cheat an Honest Man*, W. C. has to deal with labor problems, repo men, process servers, cheats—you name it.

- In *It's a Gift*, he travels cross-country to his "dream house," only to find he's been swindled.

- In *You're Telling Me*, the car bearing Sam Bisbee's puncture-proof tires has been moved only to be replaced by an identical police car, minutes before his pistol-shooting demonstration to the board of a company interested in buying his patents. He flattens all four wheels on the cop's car and then takes it on the lam.

- In *International House* he has to make a quick getaway to avoid being shot by Bela Lugosi, who thinks Fields is having an affair with Bela's ex-wife.

- In *My Little Chickadee* there was crisis both on and off the set: Cuthbert J. Twillie (W. C.) is nearly hung, and Indians attack a train while Fields verbally attacks Mae West.

Face it, things happen! And if, despite your best efforts to avoid them, bad things happen, you'd better be ready to deal with them, fast and effectively.

Companies face potential crises everyday. Some types of crisis can be avoided by active crisis-prevention planning (such as never putting Egbert Sousé on the payroll!). Others—particularly those caused by natural disasters—can't be predicted, but having plans in place should they occur can mitigate their impacts.

Smart companies don't wait for crises to arise. They take steps to prevent some types of crises and develop plans for dealing with other types of crises over which they have no control, i.e. hurricanes, earthquakes, tornadoes, etc.

Steps for Preventing and Controlling Crises

1. Appoint a crisis-management team (CMT).

2. Identify crises and develop crisis-specific prevention and response plans.

3. Identify the types of questions the media and public will ask if a particular crisis occurs and prepare answers in advance.

4. Within the CMT, identify official spokespersons and establish procedures for contacting them. (Spokespersons may be different for different types of crises.)

5. Review policies thoroughly with any and all persons likely to come in contact with the media.

6. Communicate the facts promptly to all employees. Minimize rumor and idle speculation.

7. When it's over: Review CMT procedures and outcomes. Assess how well they worked.

8. Update your CMT plan to reflect what you learned from the incident and incorporate that knowledge into your plan for future prevention/response efforts.

9. And if your canoe springs a leak and starts to sink (which happened to W. C. in *Tillie and Gus*), never take the blame, stay calm, put the causal effect on something else. It's called spin! "The river's rising!"

Crises often repeat themselves because conditions present when they first arose are not corrected. W. C. Fields actually learned that when he broke separate vertebrae in two separate bicycle accidents, these injuries often forced delays in filming or limited his scenes. Some observers have suggested that alcohol may have had a role in one or more of the incidents and suggested that he lay off the stuff. Fields probably told them, had he thought about it: "Poppycock! It's not the booze, it's the bicycles."

FIELDS IN CRISIS

There are two other Fields stories that particularly relate to crisis management. The first rule in any crisis is well known: Don't panic! On the set of *International House*, Fields and a few actors and extras were in the middle of a scene when a chandelier suddenly started to swing; then a vase and a lamp fell from a table. Earthquake! At the first tremor, a camera-man ran off the soundstage, but left the camera grinding. Consequently, we possess footage of a cool, calm Fields gently giving orders for everyone to take it easy, walk slowly, and avoid panic. He gave us a filmed version of a properly self-possessed crisis manager in action, right? A utile film showing the success of our exacting standards, right? Wrong! For more than 50 years the world believed that this bit of film showed unbelievable serenity and clear-headedness on the part of W. C. in the face of catastrophe. Then one day the director of that film came clean. It turns out everyone panicked, the day of the 1933 earthquake. The next day Fields and the director Eddie Sutherland confabbed and decided to create a promotional film that would hit the newsreels showing W. C.'s bravery—a little free publicity. They staged the whole thing less than 24 hours after the trembler. Oh well! During a crisis keeping cool, calm, and collected still works, even if you are "just kidding and pretending."

The second story involves a crisis on the set of *Tillie and Gus*—one of Fields's less successful films. One scene in the film involves a steamboat race between two rival ferryboat companies.

Just before the race began one of the steamboats started to sink. This was not part of the movie—the boat was really sinking, listing heavily on one side.

The scene was shot at Malibu Lake, a secluded little place in the Santa Monica Mountains. As the boat listed, the actors were ordered ashore and stagehands rushed aboard with buckets and began bailing water. They bailed for four hours, but the water level hadn't lowered. The fire department was called. They rushed to the scene with pumps and for five hours the pumps strained, but the water level in the boat stayed the same. Having pumped a total of nine hours, the boat's builder was called to the scene.

The director, Francis Martin, screams at the builder: "She's sinking and she's sinking fast. She's sprung a leak!"

The boat builder yawns (it was 1 A.M.) and says, "She can't spring a leak." Martin became enraged. "All I know is we've been pumping water out of her hold for nine hours and it comes in as fast as we pump it out."

The builder said: "She ain't got no hold."

Martin says he doesn't know the technical term but, "we're pumping water out of the boat's interior."

"She ain't got no interior," said the boatsman. The builder explained that the boat is more of a raft.

"She's flat on the bottom, sitting on drums. You've got all that heavy stuff on one side, and that's what makes it lean over. You've been bailing Malibu Lake into Malibu Lake for nine hours!"

W. C.'S LESSONS ON CRISIS MANAGEMENT

1. Always have a plan.

2. Don't panic!

3. Don't pump water if the boat's not leaking.

4. Avoid high-risk activities, such as riding a bicycle.

5. Don't borrow money from a bank without letting it know.

Here Charlie McCarthy brands W. C.
Branding is basically leaving your mark.
But be careful, some brands bestowed on you can actually hurt.

CHAPTER THIRTEEN

BRANDING

THERE ARE HUNDREDS OF FAMOUS COMEDIANS, but only one W. C. Fields. Both his act and his style of comedy made him a brand—and an enduring one. During his lifetime, W. C. consciously established, diligently extended, and vigorously protected his image. Procter & Gamble couldn't have done it better!

W. C. (Uncle Bill to his friends) also played an early part in the role of "product mentions," helping promote brands for Blatz beer and Chase & Sanborn coffee. (Appropriately, Charlie McCarthy once referred to W. C. as ". . . a walking ad for black coffee!") W. C. was also a walking ad for Chesterfield and Lucky Strike cigarettes. Lucky Strike sponsored the *Lucky Strike Comedy Hour* in the late thirties, featuring Fields. Their relationship did not last long, as W. C. introduced a skit featuring a fictional son, Chester. The skit was drawing weekly belly laughs, even at corporate headquarters, until an insightful

114

NEVER GIVE A
SUCKER AN EVEN
BREAK
*W. C. Fields on
Business*

brand manager at Lucky Strike finally figured it out. (Hey, if Fields has a son named Chester, then his name would be Chester Fields; you can't do that on the *Lucky Strike Hour!*)

Whether you're building a brand for your company or trying to brand yourself as a winner, Uncle Bill can help. Follow his lead and you'll soon be able to distinguish yourself from your "prairie-dogging" office neighbors, stand out from the pack, and win promotions.

Branding involves the particular association of a quality—such as reliability—with the name and symbols of a product (Coca-Cola), a manufacturer (Maytag), or a service (Federal Express). The brand is the company's assurance to consumers of particular and consistent qualities. It's also the corporate seal of authenticity, a representation to customers that they can count on the genuineness of the product or service they're buying. Branding creates an image that in most cases boosts sales and profit. Thinking of yourself as a brand can boost your career.

Successful branding is marked by four characteristics:

Consistency

The standards and qualities associated with a brand must be met consistently. Hershey's current campaign for its market-dominating chocolate bar provides a perfect example. One commercial for Hershey's shows a Little League coach trying to motivate his team. When he asks the kids if they have any questions, the precocious lot peppers him with questions about salary, endorsements, and free agency. The commercial cuts to the bottom line: "Change is bad" and follows it with the message that Hershey's great chocolate has remained "Unchanged for 100 Years!"

Charlie Chaplin had trouble making the transition from his silent-film stardom to the talking films because everyone loved his brand as the silent Little Tramp—a character that did not play well with sound. Fields, on the other hand, bombed in the silent films, but that did not matter personally because at the time he held the limelight on the Broadway stage where he attained a devoted following. He quickly became a star with the arrival of the talkies. He played specific characters: the affable, confident, albeit slightly incompetent rogue, and the browbeaten, lowly "everyman" husband who stumbled through life trying to "make-do" as he cherished hidden dreams. When Fields moved on to talking films, he hit it big right away. His loyal fans from his Broadway career knew his talking characters well and loved that brand of Fields; and for those unfamiliar with his style, they had no expectations, and thus he could introduce his well-honed brand freshly and develop a new following.

Specificity

Most successful brands are associated with specific qualities. As consumers we expect the meat in our burgers to meet USDA standards for purity. You can't build a brand around generic standards. You can, however, build a brand around the method of cooking, the appearance of the burger, and the condiments that dress it. Burger King hamburgers will always be broiled. Wendy's hamburgers are always square. McDonald's Big Mac will always come with the "special sauce" that no other burgers have.

The same types of factors apply to branding in Hollywood. Although Chaplin played other roles, the world still thinks of him as the Little Tramp. Of course Bogey reached far into different roles, but we have branded him as the tough-love Rick from Casablanca. Jackie Gleason played myriad fine roles, but the world will always brand him as Ralph Cramden. We want our stars to maintain specific signature traits, and when they don't we will ignore what we don't want to see. The same thing happens to people in business. Sometimes you cannot help the specific brand you get. But you must try to create your own "positive" brand.

Relentless Promotion

Consumers must be made aware and continually be reminded of a brand and the qualities it represents. That's why national companies spend millions each year on advertising to keep their name and qualities before the public. To avoid confusion in their messages, they make sure that all materials relating to the brand are consistently employed. Promotion is more than advertising. It extends to the design of buildings, color schemes on a letterhead, signage, and packaging—virtually in every use of a company's name, logotype, slogan, and image.

An entire industry has popped up in Hollywood of agencies that specialize in selling the names and likenesses of celebrities, or that represent the estate of celebrities from long ago. These branded celebrities are used because they have attributes that help companies sell their products and services. Fields did this in his lifetime, but his legend still grows, and he remains a marketing asset. Recently, Motorola tweaked the photo on the cover of this book to show W. C. holding his cards in one hand and a cellular phone in the other. Hershey modified the same photo of Fields, but instead of holding cards, W. C. held five Hershey bars in his hand. The reworked photo is from *My Little Chickadee* and represents one half of the Fields brand: that of a shifty, card-playing rogue. The flip side of the Fields brand comes from *David Copperfield,* in which W. C. wears a similar hat and coat, but represents the bumbling but lovable

Everyman as Mr. Micawber. Fields promoted his brands, sum-marized in these two characters, relentlessly and consistently.

Aggressive Protection

Brands must be diligently protected against encroachment. Plagiarists, rustlers, squatters, claim jumpers, counterfeiters, and detractors must be firmly (and always) challenged. If you're developing a new brand, you want to make sure it is trademarked (or servicemarked). You must see that any pro-prietary processes or equipment you use are protected by patents. You must make certain that your advertising materi-als are copyrighted. But those steps are just the beginning of your protection efforts. Once you've nailed down rights, you must actively protect them by immediately notifying infringers, encroachers, and other miscreants that specific uses require your permission. You must make sure that your marks are always used properly and the worst abusers must cease their misuse or face legal action. If they don't stop the abuse, you must take the action.

There are few newspaper reporters who have not received at one time or another in their careers letters from companies such as Kimberly-Clark, Xerox Corporation, Johnson & Johnson, and others whose trademarked product names have been commonly used to describe generic products: for exam-ple, "Kleenex" for facial tissue, "Xerox" for photocopy, and "Band-Aid" for adhesive bandage. The companies that make these and other products maintain clipping services to moni-tor the use of their brand names and send reminders to reporters and authors that their product names should not be used generically. When you order a "Coke" at a food estab-lishment that serves only "Pepsi," you're usually asked if a "Pepsi" would be okay. Both Coke and Pepsi insist on the

118

NEVER GIVE A
SUCKER AN EVEN
BREAK
*W. C. Fields on
Business*

distinction and monitor vendors to make sure customers know exactly what they're being served. (Of course, if you simply ask for a "cola," you'll get whatever's on tap—no questions asked.)

Now that you know the rudiments of branding, let's see how Fields applied them to his career.

Consistency

Once Fields had firmly established his image as the rogue, or the bumbler, or even the irascible blowhard, he fought producers, directors, and even studio heads to keep the "Everyman" image in his portrayals. Just below the surface of his irascibility or rogueries, the glint of human kindness always showed through. Indeed, when he discovered that director George Marshall left all the "pathos" in his character Larsen E. Whipsnade on the cutting-room floor, W. C. flat out refused to promote his own film *You Can't Cheat an Honest Man*. He knew his brand, his character, and he knew exactly what he wanted to project. He demanded consistency. If a radio listener knew that Fields was going to be on radio on a given evening (with or without Bergen and McCarthy), he knew what he was in for: jokes dealing with alcohol, references to his nose, tall tales, new and quotably humorous insults, the slipping in of the names of products Fields was paid to endorse—all delivered in the voice that was W. C.'s trademark. Beneath the insults and the cantankerous deliveries, a Fields audience could count on hearing a touch of human kindness in his voice. That, more than anything else, made a success out of a man who was once introduced as "anyone who hates children and dogs can't be all bad."

If you didn't like Fields's "brand" of humor, you didn't tune in. But if you liked Fields, he never failed to deliver on the promise of his brand.

Fields's image was specific. He was not just another funny-man. Here are some of Fields's "Unique Selling Propositions":

- *A unique voice.* Fields's voice was distinctively raspy, but his delivery, filled with unusual pauses and mutterings, was new to show biz. No one had talked like him before, or since.

- *A unique look.* Jimmy Durante, "The Schnozz," had the biggest and best-known nose in show biz but, in the final analysis, it was just a schnozz. Fields's "scarlet proboscis," on the other hand, was an inspiration. It wasn't just a sight gag; it was the launch point for stories on and off the screen about his childhood and his drinking. It also provided the basis for counter jabs by Charlie McCarthy: "Are you eating a tomato, or is that your nose?"

- *A unique persona.* Jack Benny was "the cheapskate." Burns & Allen were clever and zany. Will Rogers was the wise and wry hick. But only Fields made people laugh by being a curmudgeon. Fields was also unique in the way he incorporated alcohol into his acts. For example, he never portrayed a lush. His characters enjoyed their liquor, celebrated it, and castigated its opponents, much as Fields did in real life. He was neither an apologist for nor did he demean the bibulous. When asked in the film *Six of a Kind,* "Why do you drink so much?" Fields responded, "Cause I like it!"

Promotion

Fields worked to get his name before as many people as possible and to attain top billing wherever he appeared. He fre-

120

NEVER GIVE A
SUCKER AN EVEN
BREAK
*W. C. Fields on
Business*

quently sent gags to other comedians, getting a mention on their radio shows when the gags were used. And he never failed to send a thank-you note to comedians, emcees, and show hosts who mentioned him favorably. He also never failed to fire off stinging missives to those who dared debase his work. *The Christian Science Monitor,* one of the foremost detractors of W. C.'s films because of his use of alcohol, received some of his best barbs, which included the following: "Wouldn't it be terrible if I quoted some reliable statistics which prove that more people are driven insane through religious hysteria than by drinking alcohol?"

Protection

W. C. jealously guarded his acts from being copied. And he minced no words in protecting his turf. For example, in 1929, Fields was sharing the boards with Ben Blue. Blue, it seems, had a tendency to abduct other comics' material and play it as his own. Apparently, he borrowed some of Fields's material without W. C.'s permission. Shortly after Fields saw Blue's performance, the following ad appeared in the classifieds of a New York newspaper:

> *Ben Blue is a comedian in vaudeville. Ben was attacked by thugs last week near the Palace stage door. He was beaten badly. A well-known rival comic hired the ruffians. The rival, it appears, did it because Ben is supposed to have thefted his best routines and jokes.*

We do not know if it was meant as a warning or, in fact , occurred. On the other hand, we do know that Ben Blue never borrowed W. C.'s material again.

Among the best examples of W. C.'s efforts to protect his rights is his protest of the use of a double during post-production retakes of scenes in *My Little Chickadee*. On January 27, 1939, Fields complained about it in a letter to Universal's Cliff Work:

> *I am advised by my counsel that an artist whose reputation and popularity is based to a large extent upon an unusual or unique characterization has a definite interest in the manner of his portrayal and any producer who misrepresents him by the use of a double does so at his peril. Moreover, when such an artist is engaged to act in a motion picture, he has the legal right to act in that picture.*
>
> *If a producer by the use of a double of inferior ability detracts from the normal presentation of the actor it is apparent that serious injury may result to the reputation and popularity of the actor, and I do not believe that it is necessary to call to your attention that this would certainly constitute a breach of our agreement of employment on your part. . . .*
>
> *. . . Under the circumstances I must advise you that if you insist upon allowing a double to represent me in important scenes in my picture, I shall feel free to take such steps as may be necessary to protect my rights.*

Even my brothers and sister still vigorously guard W. C. Fields's brand.

W. C.'S ADVICE ON BRANDING

- Define yourself clearly—even if you have to mutter.
- Never let anyone steal your lines.
- Know that what makes you different also makes you appealing.
- No doubles allowed, except for your martinis.

NEVER GIVE A
SUCKER AN EVEN
BREAK
*W. C. Fields on
Business*

*Harold Bissonette, the poster boy for getting and keeping customers, fairly fawns all over Mr. Muckle,
the blind and deaf house detective to the hotel across the street. He wants a stick of gum
and demands that it be delivered, while he proceeds to break every bit of glassware in the store,
but Bissonette never loses his docile equanimity.*

CHAPTER FOURTEEN

GETTING AND KEEPING CUSTOMERS

As a successful comedian, W. C. Fields knew that his audience was his meal ticket. (And, with a little luck, his libations license as well.) The more capable he was of packing a house, the more houses he would be paid to pack. That meant W. C. had to deliver a consistently high level of laughter every time he performed—and he always did.

Just as great comedians keep their audiences satisfied, you have to keep your customers satisfied. In this chapter, W. C. will show you what happens when you pick the wrong customers, provide the wrong kinds of service, and offer the wrong incentives. Let's have Fields show you how *not* to do it.

In *The Pharmacist*, a short Fields did for Mack Sennett in 1933, W. C. plays Mr. Dilweg, the proud proprietor of Dilweg's Drugstore. The store gets plenty of foot traffic, but the traffic spends little if anything on Dilweg's goods. But Dilweg's business optimism never flags.

His phone rings! A customer wants some cough drops. Ah, yes, a sale! The caller wants the cough drops delivered. Sure! Dilweg takes the directions. Twenty-two miles out to the countryside! That's fine! That's why he bought that brand-new delivery truck. Customer satisfaction! The customer wants Dilweg to cut the box in half. Well, he has to draw the line somewhere.

A new customer enters the store. This guy is a grouch of the first order—looks as if he just ate a bag of lemons. Ol' Grumpy cruises the counters as Dilweg attempts to interest him in various pieces of merchandise. A book perhaps?

"Have you read *Mother India?*"

No interest!

"*The Sex Life of a Polyp?*"

No sale!

Finally, Dilweg asks, "How about a stamp? Dilweg's got a sale on those!"

(Although it's unclear in the film, an early version of the script tells us that they are two-cent stamps and that Dilweg is selling them at three for a nickel—a fact he proudly advertises on a new electronic sign he's posted outside the store.) The pharmacist holds up a sheet of stamps, hoping for a major sale. The customer, however, wants only one stamp. And he wants a black one, not a purple one. Dilweg has no purple stamps, but ever the advocate for customer satisfaction, he offers to "paint one" for the grouch. "Nah!" The customer complains, but decides he'll take the stamp anyway. Dilweg puts on his best customer-service face as he oh-so-delicately attempts to dislodge a stamp from the corner of the sheet. But the customer is persnickety. He doesn't want *a dirty* stamp; he wants a *clean* stamp, from the *middle* of the sheet.

Dilweg quickly masks his amazement and complies; after all, the customer is always right. The pharmacist snares a pair of scissors and cuts through five stamps—destroying them all—to get to the one in the middle. Dilweg then gingerly deposits the stamp in a too-large paper bag and then securely tightens the top to guard against the stamp's escape.

The customer grabs the bag and asks Dilweg if he has change for a $100 bill.

Dilweg doesn't, "But thanks for the compliment."

The customer grumbles, "Bah! I'll pay you the next time I come in!" Evidently, that's quite rare.

At least the old sourpuss doesn't want the stamp delivered!

By the end of Dilweg's day, and the short film, the only thing Dilweg has sold are cough drops to be delivered to a woman by truck 22 miles into the countryside—and we have no proof she paid.

Dilweg's approach to customer satisfaction reflects the commonly held notion that one should go to any length to attract and retain customers. You've heard variations on this theme hundreds of times: "The customer is always right!" "The customer is king." "The customer is Number 1."

While Dilweg might believe this, W. C. would, no doubt, have cried, "Taradiddle!"

Some customers may be misinformed, others dishonest, and many may simply not be worth the effort it takes to keep them happy. You don't need those kinds of customers. Instead, you need customers you *can* satisfy—and they must be customers who can satisfy *you:*

- Customers who pay their bills promptly
- Customers who let you know their changing needs

- Customers who don't begrudge you a reasonable profit

- Customers who recognize and appreciate your expertise

- Customers who will *give you* an even break to retain their business when minor dissatisfactions occur

In *The Pharmacist,* Dilweg's attempts to satisfy his customer make no economic sense (and you've seen only the tip of Dilweg's customer-service iceberg). You must do better—and, presumably, you do, or you wouldn't have been able to buy this book. But, trust us, you can do better still.

There's a three-step path for doing this:

1. Know who your current customers are.

The first step toward achieving customer satisfaction is to define the customers you have. Focus! Take a hard look at who is buying your goods or services. "Know thy customer" is second only to "Know thy limits" in terms of being successful in business.

In the days of *The Pharmacist,* most proprietors of small businesses felt they had a pretty good handle on their customer base (even if Dilweg does not). As retailing moved beyond the "Mom-and-Pop store," it became increasingly difficult for retailers to know even their customers' names, let alone their faces, lifestyles, and purchasing habits. Today it is virtually impossible for any business—even one as small as Dilweg's—to maintain customer knowledge without maintaining a computerized customer database. Such a database always records names, addresses, purchase types and frequencies, and methods of payment (cash, store card, bank card, convenience card, or even "I'll pay you the next time I come in.").

2. Pick and choose the customers you want to attract and keep.

127

CHAPTER
FOURTEEN
*Getting and
Keeping
Customers*

Your choice of customers is critical because the key to success *isn't a matter of the customer always being right,* but rather a matter *of always having the right customer.* Once you've got the right customers, pleasing them becomes a lot easier.

"Targeting the wrong customers is a very common mistake," explains Neil Baron, manager of Client Services at Sybase. "If you go after every possible customer, then you can't serve them as well as a competitor who is more focused. You have to stay focused. If you don't you'll waste a lot of time and money trying to satisfy the wrong customers."

Southwest Airlines is a perfect example. The company routinely receives some of the highest customer-satisfaction ratings in the airline industry. It does this by focusing on customers who want a fast, convenient, inexpensive way to fly. If you want filet mignon, a movie, and a massage, you won't like Southwest Airlines. But that's okay. You're not whom they have chosen to serve.

3. Control and exceed the expectations of the customers you want to keep.

Once you've chosen your customers, you have to keep them satisfied. How? Three words: exceed their expectations. It's just common sense. When you receive less than you expect, you're upset. When you receive exactly what you expect, you're happy. When you receive more than you expect, you're ecstatic.

Exceed their expectations. It sounds simple, but if it were simple, you'd hear a lot more people talking about what a great deal they got or what great service they received.

128

NEVER GIVE A
SUCKER AN EVEN
BREAK
*W. C. Fields on
Business*

Unfortunately, most people talk about just the opposite—how they got ripped off or received lousy service.

If you want to exceed customer expectations, you must first control them. You have to tell the customer exactly what to expect from you. And you've got to be certain that the expectations you set are expectations you can meet. Raising expectations can win you customers in the short term, but if you can't meet and maintain the promised level of service, you'll lose the customers you gain—and your existing customers as well.

A Ming and a Prayer

We told you earlier that you'd see only the tip of Mr. Dilweg's customer-service iceberg. Here's the rest of the story:

As the stamp-buying grouch starts to leave the pharmacy, Dilweg remembers that he has advertised a special gift for all customers: a huge, Ming-style vase. He hands one to the man, who marches out with the vase under his arm and the bag with the stamp in his hand. And, guess what? He's still frowning! And if that's not bad enough, two women enter the drugstore just to use the powder room. As they leave they remind the druggist of his vase offer. Dilweg hands each of them a vase as well! They *are* ecstatic, but they exit without buying anything.

When it comes to customer service, you can't afford to do business on a Ming and a prayer.

129

CHAPTER
FOURTEEN
*Getting and
Keeping
Customers*

 DILWEG'S CUSTOMER-SERVICE COURSE

- Some customers will never be happy, no matter what you do.
- Pursuing the wrong customers is an expensive waste of time. Be careful what you advertise: People will take you up on it.
- The customer you want is the one who will give you a break!
- When it comes to customer service, you can't afford to do business on a Ming and a prayer.

Our signature photo from My Little Chickadee! *Always remember the first rule in the Fields cannon of ethics: It is a sin to give a sucker an even break.*

CHAPTER FIFTEEN

BUSINESS ETHICS

YOU PROBABLY REALIZE BY THIS TIME THAT FIELDS looked at business with, at best, a jaundiced eye. Simon Louvish, one of W. C.'s biographers, has noted that Fields's attitudes toward business were somewhat contradictory. According to Louvish, W. C. "had no great business sense, although he cultivated his own business." W. C.'s best routines—and many of his best lines—convey a bemused mistrust of the motives, practices, and purpose of business. For example:

- Fields was meticulous in enforcing the terms of his contracts, but often protested when he was held to the letter of one himself. In fact, W. C. once said, "The best thing to break is a contract." (Certainly better than breaking your martini glass after you've just filled it!)

131

132

NEVER GIVE A
SUCKER AN EVEN
BREAK
*W. C. Fields on
Business*

- Fields made many disparaging cracks about banks and bankers, but is well known for having put small amounts of money in dozens of banks all around the world.

- He said, "Never give a sucker an even break," but W. C. guarded his off-screen reputation for being fastidiously fair with suckers and nonsuckers alike.

- He said, "You can't cheat an honest man," but believed himself to be honest and frequently felt cheated by studios and sponsors.

- He demanded (though he didn't expect) ethical behavior from his associates and competitors and behaved ethically toward them. Nonetheless, W. C. delighted in fostering his public image as a master of small-time chicanery.

- He said, "I am like Robin Hood. I take from the rich and give to the poor." When asked, "What poor?" He replied, "Us poor." In fact, Fields became a rich man, but preferred the public not know the magnitude of his wealth (he believed if people think you're rich, they won't think you're funny).

- He said, "Never smarten up a chump," but his most memorable characters—Harold Bissonette, Samuel Bisbee, Eustace McGargle, The Great McGonigle, Mr. Micawber, and Edgar Sousé—share many chumplike qualities and are played by Fields with great sympathy. Furthermore, when asked why he named one film *Never Give a Sucker an Even Break*, knowing the title would never fit on a billboard, Fields shot back, "Because I wanted the marquees to read, 'Fields . . . Sucker.'"

As a man of his times, the country's economic collapse in 1929 and the subsequent Great Depression shaped Fields's attitudes toward business (and government). They were also shaped by his early experiences in Philadelphia where he watched his father peddle old "fresh" vegetables, a practice that alerted him to the ethical ambivalence of the business world.

Although he often played a businessman and business-men appear in most of his movies, W. C. wrote only two essays that dealt specifically with business topics. One, "How to Beat a Budget," is reprinted in our chapter on budgeting. The other essay, "How to Succeed in Business," was the closing chapter of *Fields for President.*

In "How to Succeed in Business," Candidate Fields relates a tall tale claiming that shortly after the Great Crash, he is invited to dine with some of the nation's leading financial wizards. Among them, he writes, was a department-store baron who asks him for his opinion on the cause of the Depression.

"Gentlemen," Fields says, "the whole trouble is a simple and fundamental one: briefly, you have tried to sell the American people more than they could pay for."

In "How to Succeed in Business," Fields raises a number of questions about the role of ethics in business.

- Is it right to encourage people to keep on buying things when they are clearly overextended?

- Is it right to maximize the amount received from a customer based on his lack of knowledge about the terms of an offer, the use of a product, or the need of a service?

- What, if any, are the social responsibilities of a business to its community, to its employees, and to the welfare of the society in which it operates?

134

NEVER GIVE A
SUCKER AN EVEN
BREAK
*W. C. Fields on
Business*

- Do sellers have obligations to purchasers after a sale?

- Would a reduction in business taxes spawn an increase in employment?

Today's headlines are filled with stories that relate directly to these issues raised by Fields more than 50 years ago.

- Should credit-card companies be prevented from bombarding overextended consumers with more opportunities to fall deeper into debt?

- Should magazine-sweepstakes companies be required to state clearly an entry's chances of winning a prize (with or without purchase of a subscription)?

- Should manufacturers be held responsible for the economic woes a community, and employees, suffer when they relocate a plant or use massive layoffs to fatten their bottom lines?

- What liability, if any, should tobacco and firearms companies face for any ultimate harm caused by the sale of their products years before the harm occurs?

- Should corporate income, capital gains, windfall, and other taxes on business be reduced to provide an incentive for continued economic growth?

Unfortunately, corporate justifications sometimes seem grounded in Fields's contention that "anything worth having is worth cheating for." Instead of saying it as succinctly—and candidly—as W. C. did, some corporate "weasels" describe their actions in more politically acceptable terms.

- It was the lesser sin, and we had to pick one of them.

- Honorable ends justify dishonorable means.

- If I didn't do it . . . somebody would be doing it to me.

- We won, didn't we?

Such rationales are used to justify lying, credit mongering, price gouging, and other expedient ethical lapses.

ETHICAL CHEATING

Ironically, throughout his screen work—even in his cons—W. C. usually *does* give the sucker a break. For example, in *You Can't Cheat an Honest Man*, we find Larsen E. Whipsnade hustling tickets at the box office. He tricks two "dishonest" men into thinking he's given them too much change when, in fact, Whipsnade's short-changed them. Before they leave, thinking they've come out with both their tickets and some extra change, Whipsnade reiterates his circus's policy and points to a sign that bears it: "Count Your Change Before Leaving the Ticket Window. No Refunds After Leaving the Window." Now that's giving a sucker *more than an even* break! But the "dishonest" customers scurry away, hoping to get out of sight before Whipsnade can discover his "error." Later, when they realize they've been bilked, they go back to the box office to press their case for the change they were shorted. Whipsnade rebuffs them, of course: They didn't count their change before leaving the ticket window. And you can bet that Larsen E. feels no remorse for having taken them—and having taught them a rather expensive lesson.

The cons pulled by Fields's characters are minor; they are never played on the truly honest, and even when played on the dishonest, they are never played without warning. Many of his characters are basically honest, lovable rogues who play

136

NEVER GIVE A
SUCKER AN EVEN
BREAK
*W. C. Fields on
Business*

by rules that allow them only to cheat cheats but cheat them fairly. In truth, he usually depicts actions we really should never take in business. It's Fields's jaundiced view of business.

One of our favorite Fields lines dealing with ethics is found in *The Bank Dick*. A con artist, J. Frothingham Waterbury utters it when he says: "I want to prove I'm honest in the *worst* way."

Waterbury really wants to be the worst kind of *honest* man—a pretender to honesty. Most of us (and we certainly hope you're included) try to be honest in our dealings and want to work for companies and in environments that make it easy for us to remain honest. Indeed, we want to be honest in the *best* way.

Basically the guiding principle behind the dual quotes of "Never give a sucker an even break" and "You can't cheat an honest man" is be honest but don't be dumb. So let's use W. C. as our practical guide to business ethics:

- *Go ahead! Give a sucker an even break!* But only to a point. Fields shows us how in *You Can't Cheat an Honest Man*. He also did it in that famous poker scene in *My Little Chickadee*. Cuthbert J. Twillie (Fields) is running a poker game. A sucker walks up and asks if poker is a game of chance. "Not the way I play it, no," warns Twillie. The sucker sits down anyway and loses hand after hand, as Twillie takes him to the cleaners.

- *Be direct.* In *Million Dollar Legs*, the President doesn't mince his words. No obfuscations for him. He knows what's needed and says so: "What this country needs is money." And, he tells his cabinet, "It's your job to get it for me." This usually works when you're in charge.

- *Be particularly honest with yourself.* Like the men at the ticket window, if you are thrilled with the idea that you might get something you don't deserve, you're setting yourself up to be the ultimate sucker. If you believe in "get rich quick," you're primed to make someone else rich quick. Also, work to avoid some of those little lies (they always lead to bigger ones) by getting ahead of problems. For example, if you're running behind on a report, let your boss know in advance and ask for more time. In most cases, you'll get it; if the boss says "no way," you have information that will help you decide against playing that game of golf!

- *Protect yourself from the unscrupulous: Always count your change before leaving the ticket window!* There's a real advantage in calling fouls when they are committed, rather than dealing with the issue later.

On the big social issues outlined earlier, Fields would have reacted as a citizen. His lifelong fascination with the ethical foibles of humankind and his suspicious view of business would shape his continuing comment on the issues of our day—as they did in his. It would be interesting—and certainly amusing—to see what W. C. would have to say about the regulation of tobacco, alcohol, firearms, sweepstakes, credit-card solicitations, and downsizing. We suspect that as an opponent of whatever government held the reins of power, W. C. would call "Poppycock" on all government effort to protect "suckers" from their own naïve greed, ignorance, and the outcomes of their addictions. On the other hand, as someone who held Big Business in as much contempt as he held government, he might be cheering

138

NEVER GIVE A
SUCKER AN EVEN
BREAK
*W. C. Fields on
Business*

reforms that would bite the hands even of companies whose endorsement money he once gladly accepted.

One thing we know for sure: He'd make us think about the issues as he pricked the balloons of pomposity, deceit, and incompetence with his wit and his wisdom. And he'd help us get through "the brambles in our bare feet" by coining new one-liners to keep us laughing. And, we know he'd be laughing with us—all the way to those dozens of banks!

FIELDS'S ADVICE ON ETHICS AND THE ISSUES OF TODAY

- Stand clear and keep your eye on the ball!
- The only difference between a rich man and a poor man is money.
- You can fool half of the people all of the time—and that's enough to make a living.
- I am free of all prejudice. I hate everyone equally.
- Everyone must believe in something—I believe I'll have another drink!
- You can't cheat an honest man.
- Never smarten up a chump!
- Be an honest person in the *best* way! And,
- Never give a sucker an even break!

"GODFREY DANIEL!"

A Compendium of Fields Quotations and Anecdotes for All Business Occasions

ADVANCEMENT

Remember: A dead fish can float downstream, but it takes a live one to swim upstream.

The movie people would have nothing to do with me until they heard me speak in a Broadway play, then they all wanted to sign me for the silent movies.

BELIEF

A man must believe in something. I believe I'll have another drink!

BUDGETS

The last time Congress called me in to confer on the national budget, I became truly exasperated. "Gentlemen," I said, "how many times have I told you that you will never get anywhere in this matter until you purchase seven glass jars and label them (neatly): Upkeep, Interest on Debts, Running Expenses, Savings, National Defense, Seeds for Constituents, and Incidentals. If you distribute your tax intake into those jars each month, you will have the beginnings of a workable budget system—and not before!"

CHEERFULNESS

Start every day with a smile and get it over with!

CONFIDENCE

From *The Dentist*:

After throwing his golf club into the water trap, then throwing his golf bag filled with his golf clubs into the drink, Fields's golfing buddy reprimands him with, "You can't do that!"

Fields: "I can do anything I want to do!" Then he grabs his caddie and throws him into the lake!

CONTRACTS

The best thing to break is a contract.

CREATIVITY

"GODFREY DANIEL"
*A Compendium of
Fields Quotations
and Anecdotes
for All Business
Occasions*

If he [my father] had given me money to learn and to buy tricks I would have purchased a whole act, and would have had nothing original. He would not give me a cent, so I had to invent my own act and devise my own tricks.

CRISIS

[The situation] is headed for the brambles and we are all in our bare feet.

CRISIS MANAGEMENT

I like to keep a bottle of stimulant handy in case I see a snake, which I also keep handy.

Once in the wilds of Afghanistan I lost my corkscrew and was forced to live on nothing but food and water for three days.

CULTURAL DIVERSITY

. . . I have been in the entertainment business some 43 years, and I have never said anything detrimental or anything that might be construed as belittling any race or religion. I would be a sucker to do so because you can't insult the customers.

"Absolument," as they say in Hoboken.

DELEGATION

Never mind what I told you to do—you do what I tell ya'.

DEMOCRACY

Remember we are more numerous than you are.

I never vote for anyone. I always vote against.

Upon meeting the mayor of his hometown: "It's an honor, your honor. I voted for you in the last election . . . several times."

DETAIL

A comic should suffer as much over a single line as a man with a hernia would in picking up a heavy barbell.

DISCIPLINE

A man who overindulges lives in a dream. He becomes conceited. He thinks the whole world revolves around him; and it usually does.

I exercise extreme self-control. I never drink anything stronger than gin before breakfast.

According to you, everything I do is either illegal, immoral, or fattening.

THE ECONOMY

What this country needs is money!

EQUAL OPPORTUNITY

"GODFREY DANIEL"
*A Compendium of
Fields Quotations
and Anecdotes
for All Business
Occasions*

I am free of all prejudices. I hate everyone equally.

FAMILY

All the men in my family were bearded, and most of the women.

Boss: "It must be hard to lose your mother-in-law."
W. C.: "Yes, it is very hard. It's almost impossible."

FINANCE

Count your change before leaving the window.

I could only teach him how to juggle his accounts.

FOCUS

Stand clear and keep your eye on the ball!

GRATITUDE

*It was a woman who drove me to drink, and I never had the
decency to thank her.*

HEALTH AND FITNESS

I have the perfect cure for insomnia! Get plenty of sleep!

I don't believe in dining on an empty stomach.

I don't drink water; it rusts pipes.

Of course, now I touch nothing stronger than pineapple juice, 80-proof pineapple juice.

"I suffered from high blood pressure for years. Then I lost my dough and had to give it up."—Diner *in* Never Give a Sucker an Even Break, *written by Fields's pseudonym Otis Cribblecobbis.*

I don't trust doctors. Did you ever notice when doctors and morticians meet they wink at each other?

HONESTY

You can't cheat an honest man.

Con artist to Fields: "I want to prove I'm honest in the worst *way."*

IOU'S

On putting up money for a game of cut-the-cards, Fields finds himself short of the "elusive spondulix," so he proffers a substitute by writing on a small piece of paper, "I hope you'll accept my personal IOU." He lifts it up and gives it to the man, "It's worth its weight in gold."

JUSTICE

A film niece of W. C.'s seeks revenge upon bratty kids who have mocked her Uncle. She picks up a brick. Fields stops her, "No dear, do not throw that in anger. First count to ten. It will calm you. Then throw it—you'll have better aim."

KIBITZERS

They were only little snakes . . . even if they bite they wouldn't kill you.

A mother reprimanding her child for poking fun at W. C.: "You shouldn't make fun of the man's nose. Wouldn't you like a nose that big full of nickels?"

KNOWLEDGE

There comes a time in the affairs of men when you must grab the bull by the tail and face the situation.

LAWYERS

Why don't you come up and sue me sometime.

LEADERSHIP

No one likes the fellow who is all rogue, but we'll forgive him almost anything if there is warmth of human sympathy underneath his rogueries. The immortal types of comedy are just such men.

LYING

I may be a liar, but I'm a gentleman.

MARKETING

W. C.'s first encounter with a theater manager:

Manager: "How do you bill yourself?"
W. C.: "William Claude Fields, Juggler Extraordinaire!"
Manager, looking W. C. up and down: "I got it! 'W. C. Fields:
Tramp Juggler!'"

W. C. is peddling medicine oil that "Cures hoarseness! The
most stubborn case of hoarseness!" As his voice starts to
scratch, his throat constricts, his voice becomes fainter, he
chokes up, and then can't say a word. He takes a swig of his
own medicine, swallows, and, with stentorian panache, yells
"It cures hoarseness!"—creating a run on the product!

MEDIOCRITY

The harder the act, the less it seems to be appreciated. That's
what every artist, be he juggler, musician, or painter finds out.
And that is why so many mediocrities flourish—well, good luck
to them.

MOTIVATION

The reason I got into show business is because I hated to get up
in the morning, so I had to find work where I would not have
to do that.

NEGOTIATION

"GODFREY DANIEL"
*A Compendium of
Fields Quotations
and Anecdotes
for All Business
Occasions*

From a position of strength:

In It's a Gift *Fields has bought a worthless orange ranch, but he just finds out that someone wants the property to put up the grandstand for a new racetrack. His informer tells him to hold out for any price. Fields takes out a flask and starts to sip as the race-course developer approaches. The man will buy it for the price Fields paid for it, "$5,000!" "No!" Fields takes a pull on the flask.*

"$10,000."

"No!" Another gulp!

After a couple additional offers, the frustrated developer opines in anger, "You're drunk!"

W. C.: "I may be drunk, but you're crazy. I'll be sober tomorrow, but you'll be crazy for the rest of your life." And then W. C. demands $44,000 and a real *orange ranch. He gets it!*

From a position of weakness!

In My Little Chickadee *Fields (as Cuthbert J. Twillie) stands on a gallows with a rope around his neck. The executioner asks if he has any last request.*

W. C.: "I would like to see Paris before I die!"

This is rejected.

W. C.: "Philadelphia will do!"

148

NEVER GIVE A
SUCKER AN EVEN
BREAK
*W. C. Fields on
Business*

OATHS
(CERTIFIED POLITICALLY CORRECT
FOR ALL OCCASIONS!)

Godfrey Daniel!

Mother of pearl!

Balderdash!

Drat!

Suffering sciatica!

PERSEVERANCE

If at first you don't succeed, try again. Then quit. There's no use being a damn fool about it.

POLITICS

If he knows nothing else, a President should at least understand success in the business world. For, after all, what is the Presidency but a glorified business—or, at least, a fine racket?

Remember, folks, cast a vote for Fields and watch for the silver lining. Cast several votes for Fields and watch for the police.

THE PRESS

"GODFREY DANIEL"
*A Compendium of
Fields Quotations
and Anecdotes
for All Business
Occasions*

In a letter to Walter Winchell:

*Let's have a little more freedom from unjust attacks in the news-
papers for American citizens who have no power to strike back
at you or your ilk in a like manner. Less freedom of the press
and more freedom for the people from lies in the press.*

PRODUCT DEVELOPMENT

*I always made up my own acts; built them out of my knowledge
and observation of real life. I'd had wonderful opportunities to
study people; and every time I went out on the stage I tried to
show the audience some bit of true human nature.*

In The Man on the Flying Trapeze *Fields tells some friends
about the burglar-catcher chair he has invented. He explains
that when a burglar breaks into your house, you befriend him.
You offer him a drink and invite him to sit down. When the
would-be thief sits, the chair unleashes a hidden arm with a
steel ball attached. The ball swings up hitting the burglar on
the head, "Killing him instantly." During the course of the
scene, of course, Fields's character forgets about the burglar-
killer chair and sits in it. Sure enough, the steel ball cracks
Fields on the head and he is out for the count. His friends continue drinking as if nothing happened. A few minutes later
Fields comes to and realizes he is still alive. He looks at the
chair and steel ball and intones, "I'm going to have to work
on this!"*

PUNCTUALITY

I'd have been here sooner, only I got stuck on a piece of chewing gum.

QUALITY

Late in his career, Fields became concerned about the quality of his afterlife. When some friends caught him reading the Bible, they asked the notoriously antireligion comedian why he, of all people, was reading the "Good Book." Fields quietly closed the Bible and said, "Just looking for loopholes!"

RISK

Take a chance! Remember: Lady Godiva put everything she had on a horse.

Sucker: "Is this a game of chance?"
W. C.: "Not the way I play it, no."

From *The Bank Dick:*

W. C.: "Take a chance! Take it while you're young. My uncle, a balloon ascensionist, Effingham Huffnagel, took a chance. He was three and a half miles up in the air. He jumped out of the basket of the balloon and took a chance of alighting on a load of hay."

Future son-in-law: "Did he make it?"

W. C.: "Ah, no. No, he didn't. Had he been a younger man he probably would have made it. That's the point: Don't wait too long in life."

SPONTANEITY

"GODFREY DANIEL"
*A Compendium of
Fields Quotations
and Anecdotes
for All Business
Occasions*

I write my scripts short and they develop on the set, which I have found a far better premise both economically and practically.

I ad-lib most of my dialogue. If I did remember my lines, it would be too bad for me.

TAXES

The government fixes it so that you have a choice of (1) starving to death by having an income so low that you do not have to pay a tax; or (2) having an income high enough to pay a tax—and then starving to death after you've paid it.

Filling out an income-tax blank is as easy as rolling off a logarithm.

TIMING

When asked if he would be a pallbearer at John Barrymore's funeral, Fields initially declined, arguing that "the time to carry a friend around is when he's alive."

VALUES

Thou shalt not steal—only from other comedians.

You can fool half the people all of the time, and that's enough to make a good living.

I'd rather have two girls at 21 each than one girl at 42.

VISIONING

It's a wonderful thing, the D.T.s. You can travel the world in a couple of hours. You see some mighty funny and curious things that come in assorted colors.

On Mae West: What a vision of loveliness! And so well preserved too! She's a plumber's idea of Cleopatra!

It's hard to tell where Hollywood ends and the D.T.s begin.

She's all dressed up like a well-kept grave.

WARNINGS

Even a worm will turn.

Never smarten up a chump!

WEALTH

A rich man is nothing but a poor man with money.

From *Poppy:*

Fields: "I am like Robin Hood. I take from the rich and give to the poor."

Poppy: "What poor?"

Fields: "Us poor!"

"GODFREY DANIEL"
A Compendium of
Fields Quotations
and Anecdotes
for All Business
Occasions

WEASELS

I've been barbecued, stewed, screwed, tattooed, and fried by people claiming to be my friends. The human race has gone backward, not forward, since the days we were apes swinging through the trees.

What a gorgeous day. What effulgent sunshine. It was a day of this sort the McGillicuddy brothers murdered their mother with an ax.

Some weasel took the cork out of my lunch.

Why those guys [censors] won't let me do anything. They find double meaning in commas and semicolons in my scripts.

WILLPOWER

Now don't say you can't swear off drinking; it's easy. I've done it a thousand times.

I exercise extreme self-control. I never drink anything stronger than gin before breakfast.

WORKAHOLICS

If ants are so busy, why do they attend so many picnics?

WORRY

Never cry over spilt milk, because it may have been poisoned.

I have a fine heart . . . it will last me as long as I live.

YOU

Don't be a fuddy-duddy! Don't be a mooncalf! Don't be a jabbernowl! You're not one of those, are you?

FILMOGRAPHY

The films listed here were in general release on videotape when this book went to press. Other Fields films are rereleased periodically. For the latest available offerings, check with your favorite source of videos for sale or rental. We've rated each film with one to four martini glasses, indicating their entertainment value.

W. C. Fields: Six Short Films (1915–1933) ♇♇

VHS/DVD   B&W   112 minutes

This collection features six short films by Fields, including the silent *Pool Sharks* (1915) and Fields's first sound film, *The Golf Specialist* (1930). We give these only a vodka martini each—they're for serious Fields fans only. Mack Sennett produced the other four shorts on this tape. Three of the Sennett shorts—*The Dentist*, *The Barber Shop*, and *The Pharmacist*, rate four martinis each. The last short, *The Fatal Glass of Beer*, doesn't have much in the way of management lessons, but it does feature one of Fields's best-known lies: "And it ain't a fit night out for man nor beast!" That bit alone is worth a couple of martinis. The collection also shows off the work of many supporting players who worked extensively with W. C., including Elise Cavanna, Grady Sutton, Joe Bordeaux, and Babe Kane. The short *His Lordship's Dilemma*, 1915, is lost.

156

NEVER GIVE A
SUCKER AN EVEN
BREAK
*W.C. Fields on
Business*

The Bank Dick (1940) ΥΥΥ

VHS/DVD   B&W   74 minutes

Fields wrote the script, under the pseudonym Mahatma Kane Jeeves, for this classic in which he plays the beleaguered Edgar Sousé, who winds up with a job as a bank security officer after taking credit for foiling a bank robbery. Considered by many to be Fields's best screen comedy. Watch the cast for appearances by Shemp Howard (as the bartender) and the inimitable Franklin Pangborn as the bank examiner. Directed by Eddie Cline.

The Big Broadcast of 1938 (1938) ΥΥ

VHS/DVD   B&W   90 minutes

Dorothy Lamour, Bob Hope, Shirley Ross. This is one of those Hollywood set pieces in which the studios show off their stars in a lamely framed plot. This one involves two brothers, both played by W. C.—one successful, one a failure—who own a steamship line. Two liners—the *Colossal* and the *Gigantic*—are engaged in a transatlantic race from New York to London. The voyage allows plenty of time for vignettes by Bob Hope (his first feature film—and his first recording of "Thanks for the Memories"), Dorothy Lamour, Martha Raye, Kirsten Flagstad (singing Wagner), and a half-dozen lesser lights enjoying their Hollywood minutes of fame. Directed by Mitchell Leissen.

David Copperfield (1935) ΥΥΥΥ

VHS/DVD   B&W   130 minutes

One of the great movies of the 1930s, Fields got top billing for his portrayal of the eternally hopeful Mr. Micawber. Though his role is relatively minor, Fields delivers the finest dramatic performance of his career. He deserved at least an Academy Award nomination for Supporting Actor, but didn't get one. The rest of the cast is superb: Basil Rathbone, Una O'Connor, Lionel

Barrymore, Edna May Oliver, Elsa Lancaster, Maureen O'Sullivan, and Freddie Bartholomew, among many other fine stars. *David Copperfield* is a remarkably faithful adaptation of Dickens's novel—particularly for its time. Not to be missed. We'd give it five martinis, but we've run out of gin. Directed by George Cukor.

International House (1933) 🍸🍸🍸🍸

VHS   B&W   70 minutes

World powers are racing to Shanghai to bid on rights to a television device invented by a Chinese scientist. Fields, as the high-flying Professor Quail, drops into the midst of things and is mistaken for the American delegate to the auction. A celebrity-studded cast, featuring Peggy Hopkins Joyce (famous in her day for having married a lot of rich men), Stuart Erwin, Bela Lugosi, Cab Calloway, Sterling Holloway, Rudi Vallee, George Burns, Gracie Allen, and Baby Rose Marie—they all get their moments in the sun in this vehicle for their acts. Directed by A. Edward Sutherland.

It's a Gift (1934) 🍸🍸🍸🍸

VHS/DVD   B&W   73 minutes

Fields, as Harold Bissonette (pronounced "biss-oh-nay" in front of Mrs. Bissonette), shows you how to handle a successful negotiation and how not to cater to customers. He plays a small-town grocer who dreams of packing up his family and buying an orange grove in California. The cast includes Jean Rouveroul, Baby LeRoy, Kathleen Howard, and Jane Withers. Directed by Norman Z. McLeod.

Million Dollar Legs (1932) 🍸🍸

VHS   B&W   64 minutes

Klopstokia, a small European country, decides to enter the Olympics as a means of boosting its tourist economy. Turns out

158

NEVER GIVE A
SUCKER AN EVEN
BREAK
*W.C. Fields on
Business*

all of Klopstokia's citizens posses remarkable athletic powers, including Fields, who plays the President of Klopstokia. The President is a strongman, as in dictator, but is also a strongman as in "he can hoist 1,000 pounds!" The script, written in part by Joseph Mankiewicz, is modern in concept, but the dialogue is often stilted. Still, an innovative and interesting film for its time, full of great lines and more than a couple of management-lesson launch points. It's the Olympics equivalent of *The Mouse that Roared*. Directed by Edward Cline.

My Little Chickadee (1940) ☍ ☍

VHS/DVD   B&W   83 minutes

Fields and Mae West team up in the Old West, where he's an itinerant flimflam man and she's a madam who has been run out of one town and hopes to set up in the next. Filled with great one-liners for both leads, who shared screenwriter credits, we gave it a glass a piece for W. C. and Mae. The show was a box-office success, but a critical bomb. The real story was taking place behind the scenes, where West and Fields were at war over credits, scenes, and lines. The rest of the cast includes Joseph Calleia, Margaret Hamilton, Robert Foran, and Fuzzy Knight. Directed by Edward Cline.

Never Give a Sucker an Even Break (1941) ☍ ☍ ☍

VHS/DVD   71 minutes

Fields's last starring role. The plot puts Fields in front of a skeptical studio head during a typical "pitch" session in which W. C. tries to sell his screenplay concept. As he tells it, and while the studio head rejects it, we actually see the improbable "screenplay" become the movie within the movie. Despite its disjointedness—or perhaps because of it—the film shows Fields in some of his finest screen moments. The rest of the cast is strong: Gloria Jean, Margaret Dumont, Leon Errol, and Franklin Pangborn. Directed by Edward Cline.

Running Wild (1927) 🍸🍸🍸

VHS   B&W/Silent   68 minutes

Hilarious silent feature is a must for Fields fans. After being hypnotized, then-mustachioed Fields is transformed from a shy, beleaguered husband–father into a fearless, outgoing, and humorously nasty master of the house. Believing he is a lion, Fields makes life unbearable for his unreasonable boss and over-bearing wife. The cast includes Mary Brian, Claude Buchanan, and Marie Shotwell. Directed by Gregory La Cava.

Sally of the Sawdust (1925) 🍸🍸

DVD   B&W/Silent   91 minutes

Fields is a sideshow juggler (and con man) who works to restore his ward to her proper place in society after she falls in love with a rich young man. This was later remade as *Poppy*. Stars Carol Dempster, Alfred Lunt, and Ervill Anderson. Extensive footage of Fields's spectacular juggling routines. Directed by D. W. Griffith.

Six of a Kind (1934) 🍸🍸🍸

VHS   B&W   62 minutes

This is a fine film with a great cast that includes George Burns, Gracie Allen, Charlie Ruggles, and Mary Boland. Fields plays Sheriff "Honest John" Hoxley and shoots a little pool when he's encountered by George and Gracie and Charlie and Mary, who are driving themselves crazy as they drive cross-country. Directed by Leo McCarey.

Tales of Manhattan (1942) 🍸

VHS/DVD   Color   118 minutes

Fields's performance was brief and his scene was deleted from the original theatrical release, though restored in later editions.

160

NEVER GIVE A
SUCKER AN EVEN
BREAK

*W.C. Fields on
Business*

All-star cast includes Charles Boyer and Rita Hayworth. Directed by Julien Duvivier.

Fields's recently restored skit ♟♟♟♟ of *Tales of Manhattan*

You Can't Cheat an Honest Man (1939) ♟♟♟

VHS/DVD   B&W   76 minutes

Fields, as Larson E. Whipsnade, manages a down-at-the-tentpoles traveling circus. He has to deal with a social-climbing son, disgruntled performers, and sheriffs in pursuit. Lots of nonsense, great one-liners, and a great cast that includes Edgar Bergen and Charlie McCarthy, Constance Moore, Grady Sutton, and Eddie "Rochester" Anderson. Whipsnade may shortchange the suckers at the ticket office, but Fields gives full value to his audiences. Directed by George Marshall (but Eddie Cline directed most of Fields's scenes).

You're Telling Me (1934) ♟♟♟♟

VHS   67 minutes

Fields plays Samuel Bisbee, optician, dreamer, inventor, and toper. He's embattled at home, doesn't bring home enough money, but, at last, comes up with a truly workable invention—a puncture-proof tire. His first attempt to sell it is a disaster until he befriends, without knowing who she is, a European princess. In the end, he licenses his invention, gets rich, establishes himself at the top of the social set (thanks to the princess's help) and finds himself head of a happy family. A fairy tale of the highest order. And, funny—we're telling you! Cast includes Buster Crabbe, Joan Marsh, Kathleen Howard, Louise Carter, and the strikingly beautiful Adrienne Ames. Directed by Erle C. Kenton.

Other Fields films that have been or may be released in the future:

SILENTS

Janice Meredith (1925)

That Royal Girl (1925)

It's the Old Army Game (1926)

So's Your Old Man (1926)

The Potters (1927)

Two Flaming Youths (1927)

Twillie's Punctured Romance (1928)

Fools for Luck (1928)

SOUND

Her Majesty Love (1931)

If I Had a Million (1932)

Hip Action (short—1933)

Hollywood on Parade B-2 (1933)

Tillie and Gus (1933)

Alice in Wonderland (1933)

Hollywood on Parade B-10 (1934)

162

NEVER GIVE A
SUCKER AN EVEN
BREAK
*W.C. Fields on
Business*

The Old-Fashioned Way (1934)

Mrs. Wiggs of the Cabbage Patch (1934)

Mississippi (1935)

Man on the Flying Trapeze (1935)

Poppy (1936)

The Laziest Golfer (1942)

Follow the Boys (1944)

Song of the Open Road (1944)

Sensations of 1945 (1944)

INDEX

164

NEVER GIVE A
SUCKER AN EVEN
BREAK
*W. C. Fields on
Business*

168

NEVER GIVE A
SUCKER AN EVEN
BREAK
*W. C. Fields on
Business*